A Romantic Look at Norwich School Landscapes by a Handful of Great Little Masters

Peter Kennedy Scott

The Cottage Children. Oil on oak panel.
JB Ladbrooke, c1835
22 x 19 ins., 56 x 48.3 cms.
The Norwich School will always be known for its
trees and by its trees, featuring the influence of
Dutch 17th century painting on Crome and pupil
alike.

Published by Acer Art Publishing 1998
19-23 Fore Street, Ipswich IP4 1JW

Design and production by Raymond Grisby, Lincoln

A CIP catalogue record for this title is available from
the British Library

ISBN 0 9534711 0 1 Hardback
ISBN 0 9534711 1 X Paperback

Origination and printing by
The Journal Printing Company, Scunthorpe

Acknowledgements

A WHILE AGO a handful of friends suggested that I should record some notes or even write a book about the Norwich School. I can only say that without their encouragement and the help of museums, auction houses, galleries and libraries and a considerable number of collectors the completion of this book could not have taken place.

My foremost thanks must go to Norma Watt, Assistant Keeper of Art at the Norwich Castle Museum who, with Andrew Moore, Keeper, allowed access to research material over a long period of time, with Norma Watt freely giving advice on many detail and historical points. I am also grateful to the Print Rooms of the British Museum and the Victoria & Albert Museum for their assistance in research.

Some two dozen sources have been used from which the illustrations have been amassed. Many of these have been private collections; I am exceedingly grateful to the owners who so readily allowed their pictures to be photographed and reproduced here. Two of the most important subjects belonged to Nestlé UK Ltd. Where a museum has allowed a painting to be illustrated an acknowledgement will be found beneath it. Nearly all the photography has been carried out by Curtis Lane & Co. of Sudbury, Suffolk, which was not without its problems on location – camera dodging a low-slung chandelier or side-stepping a Norwich Terrier! Four museums have kindly supplied the remaining photographs; where this has happened the fact is also mentioned in the caption. The photographic department of the V&A was particularly helpful in carrying out difficult work on a dilapidated sketchbook.

The Witt Library of the Courtauld Institute was used extensively for reference into English and Continental paintings – the vast collection of fully documented photographs proving invaluable. Likewise a number of auction houses have provided easy access to see paintings 'en passage'. These include Sothebys, Christies, Phillips (E Anglia), Bonhams and the Norfolk firm of GA Key. Art galleries have provided a source of study. Ackermann and Johnson (formerly Oscar and Peter Johnson) in London and Mandell's Gallery in Norwich deserve special mention for their production of detailed exhibition catalogues, quite apart from their displays of 19th century East Anglian art. Credit must also go to Rowans Gallery in Norfolk.

Finally I must thank the Haags Gemeentemuseum, its Printroom, and the Haags Historisch Museum in Holland for their help in allowing visits to view material incorporated into the chapter on the Continental connection. John Sillevis, Curator of the Gemeentemuseum, kindly consented to the reproduction of a painting under his care.

All the opinions expressed in this book, hopefully along the right lines, are my own, except where specifically stated otherwise. Needless to say I am grateful to many friends and acquaintances who have guided me along a difficult track – trying to separate the wood from the trees in many a Norwich School jungle!

Christmas 1977

In the Bleak Mid-Winter... long ago
Pencil and monochrome.
CJW Winter, signed
7 x 9 ins., 17.8 x 22.8 cms.

Contents

Near Plumstead Old Church, Norfolk. Oil on oak panel.
H Bright. Initialled HB, dated (18)29, inscribed and
signed on reverse
5 1/4 x 7 ins., 13.3 x 17.8 cms.
*The influence of Alfred Stannard in this and the
river scene is dramatic. Not only do these
paintings reveal the influence he had on Bright's
early work but also that Bright was apprenticed to
Stannard by the age of 19 and probably had been
so for a while. Furthermore, some of the make-up
of this painting appears in one of Stannard's
early works. It can now be said the figures already
show Bright's colour style as does the band of
brightness before the trees, but, without initials
and the provenance of the other, his name could
have proved difficult to come by. Note the Norman
round tower – the church is dedicated to St
Protase and St Gervase.*

Trees by River with Cattle. Oil on oak panel. **H Bright**
5 1/8 x 7 ins., 13 x 17.8 cms.
*This unsigned painting forms a pair with the
other small oil of Plumstead Church by Bright.
The river scene is illustrated in M Allthorpe-
Guyton's revised book on Henry Bright with the
comment that it was Bright's earliest known
painting, having come into the Castle Museum's
possession in 1982 through descent from a niece
of the artist. However, fifteen years on, it now
vies for this position with the signed and dated oil
that has just surfaced from another collection.
(Reproduced and photographed by courtesy of
Norfolk Museums Service)*

Introduction

THE POETRY OF PAINTINGS has long caught the imagination. Why else are picture galleries so often full if it is not for their magic pull? The Norwich School, as a group, romanticised country scenes in the nineteenth century in a way not seen before. Now the effect, one hundred and fifty years on, is all the more remarkable. As bystanders we gaze back on simple views of rural life and no doubt feel refreshed, temporarily released from modern life, by their colourful tranquillity.

Perhaps we can imagine, those many years ago, what life was like in this part of England where the city of Norwich had stood for centuries. In the quiet countryside the familiar noises came from farm animals. What mechanical sounds there were came from windmill sails revolving at work, or cartwheels crunching on stones. Often the only smoke to stain the sky arose from bonfires, camp fires or chimney pots – as 'Norwich' pictures portrayed with gypsy groups or cottage scenes. The weather sang its own tune in the woods and trees and broke branches on bad days, just as it ever did, for the painters to record. Maybe it was a quiet life, but it was likely to have been a hard one, for living off the land, or the sea , was the essence of survival for many. The industrial revolution, which embraced the cotton mill cities of the Midlands and the

Lane scene near Sheringham. Oil on Panel. **J Stark**
22 x 30 ins., 55.9 x 76.2 cms.
This view, by tradition, has been given this title. Half a dozen versions exist, including this up till now unrecorded one. The village in the distance may represent Upper Sheringham. Country folk camping (with a donkey) was a feature of Stark's Norwich period, which this so evidently is, and his later Windsor one. He did other variations of this tree group in his Postwick Grove scenes. The standing figure is very much a 'Stark' man, dressed accordingly. This picture, so typical of the Norwich School, shows Stark with his Dutch and quite heavy style of early woodland painting, circa 1820.

North, along the spine of Britain, though it touched Norwich, of course, hardly affected the rural scene of East Anglia. It was not until a century on that the combine harvester crept into the fields, sweeping aside some of the landscapes so cherished by the Norwich School. And in a different way the city of Norwich itself developed, swamping the bracken and gorse heathlands of Mousehold where 'John Crome's' much-painted windmill had stood for years in open country. The unspoilt sight before the eyes of the Norwich School painters is what we see in their paintings today.

This was their stage. If it was not the lanes and woodlands then the flat landscape of East Anglia, dotted with timber-framed houses, flint churches and windmills, with a wherry on a river here and there, under long skies branded by broad sunsets, supplied the ingredients peculiar to the Norwich School's success. The artists began to enjoy enhancing the natural views they saw, adding a variety of light and colour. By so doing a new school of painting was seen to evolve which was appealing and therefore attractive to students. This is perhaps why it became the principal provincial school of painting of its time. Although the landscape artists were recording nothing more than rural scenes and life, it is by the manner they achieved this that no other school probably evokes quite such a nostalgic response.

There is little doubt that the Norwich School was popular in its heyday, judging from its output which was clearly considerable. Helped by its size it became culturally important with its public exhibitions and growing private collections. Over the years many artists worked in Norwich or within travelling distance of the city, and many others sent paintings from further afield, from London even, to these exhibitions. In the Norwich Society's own thirty year history, the first 'life' of the school, more than five hundred artists exhibited. So, for the purpose of this book and to simplify the study of the school, selecting a list that is limited to the fifty best known names covering three generations of painters, whose working lives altogether span much of the nineteenth century, is a difficult task. Some might say that it is impossible; however a certain undeniable core of names stands out, some forty or so, and the best of the rest, who may be only loose associates, has to be included in this arbitrary list. Together they form an accepted group of recognised artists; this book sets out to look at the works of one half of this group.

Much of the work of the school was comprised of sketches, though most people today are far more familiar with the fully worked-up paintings. It will be seen that there is a mixture of both, but there is a greater emphasis than is usual in a book of this kind towards the oil sketches showing the easy excellence some artists achieved in this sphere – when not faced with the more formal task of completing a major studio painting. Sometimes only one or two illustrations have been used for a familiar artist; on other occasions the opportunity has been taken to expand on certain painters with many new examples, so providing a fresh insight into their working ways. This it is hoped will promote a further interest in the school. Needless to say, in a short book, it is only possible to skim the surface collecting a few representative samples from possibly thousands. However, one or two unlikely surprises are also included adding spice to the study. Probably all the artists of the school painted landscapes at some time, since, for the majority, this was their main artistic occupation. But it should not be overlooked that a sizeable minority specialized in seascapes and still life, in particular, and townscapes and portrait painting too – subjects that are not within the scope of this book.

OVERLEAF PAGE 12
Wooded Landscape. Oil on canvas. **JB Crome**
40 x 50 ins., 101.6 x 127 cms.
*This large picture demonstrates the School's
ability to produce landscapes of some size. The
scene is basically the same as that painted by
JBC, View near Bury St Edmunds, 1832 (Castle
Museum Coll.). The illustrated picture may have
been painted as a full-scale study for the Bury
version which has a culvert in the bank, through
which the stream flows, and a detailed distant
view with a windmill on a hill. JBC's tree
painting can be easily studied here; and so can
the group of wild flowers – in one corner – which
is similar to that often painted by George Vincent
with whom he worked. The curling sky is likewise
not unlike Vincent's. The distinctive style of figure
painting is worth noting.*

For most people, the product of the school, rather than its history, is of far more interest, but one does not belong without the other. Many books have already rendered useful and detailed histories which can easily be referred to, on Crome and Cotman in particular. The principal purpose of this book is to concentrate on a whole range of landscape views not hitherto published in a book of this kind, bar a small handful which are included for their particular relevance. The second objective is to discuss many of these paintings, alongside their artists, to see how they fit together and into the working pattern of the Norwich School. This may not add much to the history of the school but the more serious analysis may bring a better understanding of certain artists and the concept of the term 'Norwich School'. As so many paintings of the school are unsigned the further purpose of this analysis will become apparent. Furthermore, the Norwich School is not looked at in isolation as its close links at home are examined, and illustrated, as well as those on the nearby continent – expanding the field of study into a wider area of interest.

A search is always on for more paintings to peruse and for more information about the artists. Each time another picture is found and identified the school reveals more of its secrets and its past. Judging from the volume of material that has appeared during the last thirty years there is much more yet to come.

The last of the Norwich School landscape painters, who knew Old Crome, died exactly one hundred years ago. This was also the year in which the publication of the first collective book on the Norwich School, albeit confined to Crome and Cotman, appeared. William Philip Barnes Freeman, who came from a well respected Norwich family, connected with the offices of mayor, painter and frame maker, knew John Crome when he, William, was a young boy. He died in 1897 in the same year that Laurence Binyon, the art historian and poet, produced the first book about Norwich artists. *A Romantic Look at Norwich School Landscapes*, a century on, is a tiny tribute to the landscape painters of the school and their study, which it is hoped, will inspire many more to see the merits of a most important English and, indeed, European school of art.

Costessey Hall. Oil on board. **WPB Freeman**
4 5/8 x 8 1/4 ins., 11.7 x 20.9 cms.
*This view was painted by other artists
(e.g. Thirtle) and shows the hall before later
demolition. The shaft of woodland light was a
Freeman feature, so too was his spotty foliage by
which he can be identified. In an untypical way
he concentrated on blocks of thick bushy tree-
forms, shifting away from the earlier Norwich
idiom of woods comprised of individual trees.*

Homestead. Oil on panel. **G Vincent**, monogrammed, and dated 1813(?)
8 ¹/₂ x 7 ¹/₄ ins., 21.6 x 18.4 cms.
This early study by Vincent shows the detail of his foliage and the dots of flower colour. Note the trees built on spindly trunks and the construction of his early clouds. Cows painted by the Ladbrookes, Stark and Vincent and others can be usefully compared.

One
History of the
Norwich School

The painters · Norwich and Norfolk
The Norwich Society and exhibitions

OVERLEAF
Norwich. Pencil drawing. **JB Ladbrooke**
Illustration from sketchbook. (ref. E907–1928)
5 3/4 x 9 3/8 ins., 14.6 x 23.8 cms.
Reproduced with photograph kindly supplied by the Victoria & Albert Museum

FACING PAGE TOP
Pony Feeding in a Village Yard.
Pencil and Watercolour. **J Thirtle**
10 x 14 ins., 25.4 x 35.7 cms.
This village scene, on 'Oatmeal' paper (c 1820), dates to Thirtle's more colourful and later period – a red jacket on a man and a sandy-yellow cottage wall. He often repeats the idea of a building filling one side of a painting. An inscription on the reverse reads 'John Sell Cotman?' – the style of Cotman not only influenced Thirtle but also the owner of the picture!

FACING PAGE BOTTOM
Water Gate, Lower Close, Norwich. Watercolour on paper board. **J Thirtle**
11 1/4 x 15 1/2 ins., 28.6 x 39.4 cms.
This view is another version of the slightly less detailed watercolour in the V&A of a similar size which Thirtle exhibited in 1810. Through the flat archway, and over the roofline, masts of the boats lying off Pull's Ferry are visible. Thirtle frequently painted wherries. Mousehold Heath, with ruined St Leonards Abbey, lies on the horizon. The buildings are worth studying for Thirtle's fine detail of brick and tile. Water once flowed through the 'gate' into the 'close' before it was all filled in.

THE NORWICH SCHOOL became not only the main provincial school of painting of its time, but also the one with the longest life. Its original styles combined to form a cornerstone on which landscape painting of the nineteenth century developed. The school was born when the Norwich Society was founded. In fact, if it had not been for this society, the school might never have become an entity expanding around the society and then growing after its demise.

In 1803 John Crome, with old friends such as Robert Ladbrooke, formed a small society. Fortnightly meetings commenced with the study of prints, drawings and casts. Of secondary importance, then, were the annual exhibitions which began in 1805. However, during its lifetime it was destined to hold some thirty exhibitions.

When the society was disbanded, in 1833, further exhibitions were held to which local artists contributed so long as they could paint, for a further forty-five years. These artists, together with former society exhibitors, formed the group which painted so prodigiously as to acquire the title in later times of 'Norwich School'.

THE PAINTERS

It may seem strange that so many artists came to develop their skills in Norwich around the same time. It is therefore worth looking at how this happened and how so many artistic families became linked.

John Crome, father of the Norwich School, was born in 1768 and **John Sell Cotman** in 1782. Their styles of painting were to develop quite differently, with the Crome one predominating in the school. The next important name to consider is **Robert Ladbrooke**. He was born in 1769 and became a great friend of John Crome. Not only did he and Crome surely paint together but they married into the same family, wedding a Berney sister each. These two couples then produced a string of artists with their mothers' maiden name attached to a son apiece. **John Berney Crome** and **William Henry**, his brother, together with **Henry** and **John Berney Ladbrooke** will all be seen to feature in this book. Robert Ladbrooke married a second time, after the death of his first wife Mary, and from this union **Frederick Ladbrooke** appeared. All in all the two families account for no less than seven artists.

John Sell Cotman was born in Norwich, and so too was **John Thirtle**, in 1777, who became an artist of considerable repute under the influence of Cotman. Thirtle was a famed frame maker besides. These two artists found themselves marrying sisters by the family name of Miles. John Sell had several children, two of whom became well known, **Miles Edmund** and **John Joseph Cotman**. The tie between these two families accounts for another four artists.

Robert Ladbrooke is known to have taught **Joseph Stannard** to paint but, even so, he developed a style of his own, much to his credit. Joseph was born in 1797 and married Emily Coppin, who, as **Mrs Joseph Stannard**, became a spirited and fine painter of still life. Joseph's brother **Alfred** was born in 1806 and followed in his brother's footsteps producing some landscapes of stunning quality, together with seascapes. He married in 1827, and very soon afterwards **Alfred George Stannard** and his sister **Eloise Harriet**, so well known for her still life paintings of flowers and fruit, were born to become later members of the school.

An early member to be born in Norwich was **James Sillett** in 1764, who likewise painted still life and landscapes. Five years later **Charles Hodgson** was born in Norwich

FACING PAGE TOP
Woodland Glade. Oil on millboard (Winsor and Newton). **A Priest**
6 x 8 7/8 ins., 15.2 x 22.5 cms.
This sketch was painted perhaps after Priest's return to Norfolk in 1848, certainly after 1841 judging by the label on the back. He completed many small, and even tiny, colourful landscapes. The palette is not unlike A Sandys', to whom this painting was once attributed, but the sky is not typical of him. His double tree mass is a distinguishing feature.

FACING PAGE BOTTOM
Norfolk Cottage by a Pond. Oil on canvas. **A Priest**
20 x 32 ins., 50.8 x 81.3 cms.
This late-in-life painting is a pleasant blend of trees, clouds and cottage, clay-lump perhaps. Splashes of white on the branches mark Priest's work. His tree masses were often split in two with an avenue to a distant view. The sky is worth noting: boldly divided into blue and white with rounded cloud forms. The canvas was unstretched for 150 years being supported instead by a large print of the Earl of Leicester!

too, and became a painter exhibiting works with the Norwich Society. His son **David**, who is best remembered for his colourful townscapes, was born in 1798. His daughter **Anna** married Alfred George Stannard, thereby loosely linking the Hodgson and Stannard families.

Other individual artists appeared at different times. **Henry Ninham**, son of **John Ninham**, who probably taught him to paint, was born in 1796 and, like David Hodgson, painted architectural subjects. **James Stark**, a prolific landscape painter and a pupil of John Crome, was also born in the city two years earlier. He was later to greatly influence **Samuel David Colkett** several years younger than him, and his son **Arthur James Stark**.

Continuing with this list, which is perhaps the easiest way to categorise the formation of the school, **Alfred Priest** started life in 1810. He later moved to London and became a pupil of James Stark. One painter, who was also taught by a different generation of artists, was **John Middleton**, a pupil of JB Ladbrooke. Middleton, a brilliant watercolourist, was born in Norwich in 1827 but only enjoyed a short life. This was so of one of the more famous artists **George Vincent** too, who was born two years after Stark and only lived until he was thirty-five.

The Joy brothers are often associated with the Norwich School, and rightly so. They were born in Yarmouth at the turn of the century and exhibited in Norwich for many years before moving away to Portsmouth. **Edwin Cooper** moved from Bury St Edmunds, where he was born, to Beccles and exhibited with the society from 1806 onwards. A year earlier **Robert Dixon** began exhibiting after settling in Norwich. **CJW Winter** lived at Bungay until he moved to Yarmouth and, like Cooper, he painted horses and dogs in landscape settings. **Joseph Clover** came from Aylsham. The Freeman family has already had a mention.

Other painters appeared in Norwich like **Thomas Lound** and **Henry Bright**, who was born in Suffolk, and **Robert Leman** who was influenced by Bright. Another newcomer to the city was **Anthony Sandys** from rural Norfolk who, in particular, carried on the Crome tradition.

This list is not exhaustive but tries to embrace most of the Norwich School's better known names. Paintings by these artists span much of the century, with JB Ladbrooke dying in 1879 and A Sandys in 1883. **Obadiah Short** lived until 1886. He was born in Norwich the same year as JB Ladbrooke, whose influence shows in some of his work. Alfred Stannard died after out-living his son, but his daughter lived on into the twentieth century – well beyond the life of the school.

NORWICH AND NORFOLK

In the seventeenth century Norwich was second to London in terms of population – it was a large important city of its time. It had enjoyed a Dutch influence in its earlier development with many Dutch-speaking people inhabiting the city. This connection with the Continent was to play an important part in Norwich's fortunes, commercially and artistically.

The wealth that the capital of East Anglia was to create depended on its trade with the outside world. Textiles were England's chief export in the eighteenth century. Norwich worsted and lightweight coloured cloths, known as 'Norwich Stuffs', came to be manufactured in increasing quantities and exported abroad so that, by the mid-

FACING PAGE TOP
House in the Trees. Monochrome. **W Joy**
8 x 12 ins., 20.3 x 30.5 cms.
This early monochrome shows many similarities to the 'Felbrigg' Joy with its foliage, bare twigs and branches and was probably painted in his childhood too. It comes from the same collection as the Felbrigg view and is similar to others in the Great Yarmouth Museum.

FACING PAGE BOTTOM
Lake at Felbrigg Park. Watercolour. **W Joy**
6 ⅝ x 9 ⅜ ins., 16.9 x 23.9 cms.
'In Felbrigg Park, July 24 1816 WJ' is inscribed on the reverse of the mounting paper which itself is a piece of Whatman paper, watermarked 1812, removed from a sketch book. This watercolour view of the lake shows the competence of William Joy at the age of 13. It is possible he had travelled from Yarmouth to visit relatives as an estate map of 1830, though a few years later, shows a Joy family living there. He is known to have painted a fair number of landscapes including a large oil of the Broads. The point from which he took his view is rather overgrown today, but the park cattle 'water' just the same. The rounded clouds are often seen in his more familiar seascapes. It was in the Park church that JS Cotman married Ann Miles in 1809, not ten minutes' walk from the lake.

eighteenth century, there was an enormous trade in textiles not only to the Continent but to other parts of the world. Much of the wool for this fine worsted came from nearby Lincolnshire, whereas for the large leather-working industry the cattle grazed in the rich river valleys around Norwich and Yarmouth. Besides being famous for its cattle market Norwich was noted for its trade in farm produce, corn and clover seeds, and in particular for its first class barley for its big brewing industry.

Such was the volume of commerce that it led to the development of the banking and insurance businesses in the city, of which the Norwich Union is the best known. This was founded at the end of the eighteenth century. The ability to create wealth received something of a setback during the Napoleonic wars when trade with the Continent declined considerably. (On the positive side the French Revolution caused an influx of paintings from many parts of the Continent, incidentally creating the basis for an art market in London). Moreover, other cities had easily overtaken Norwich in terms of population and industrial might. However this does not mean to imply that there was not by then a certain number of families and individuals enjoying a wealthy status – all at a time when John Crome and his fellow painters were entering the frame.

For a long time, scenically, Norwich had lent itself to painting. It boasted a beautiful cathedral dating back to the eleventh and twelfth centuries and over fifty parish churches. It enjoyed lively markets in its streets. The River Wensum meandered through Norwich where the famous wherry, now born in these times, plied. The wherry could ferry goods along the Yare to Yarmouth where larger sea going boats were harboured. Norwich was blessed with a navigable river which allowed for such trading opportunities. In its pretty streets many of the delightful timber-framed houses were occupied by merchants.

At the same time, dotted around the countryside, within reach of Norwich, were a number of wealthy families. Indeed old maps of the county show many estates both small and large with some set in magnificent parks. As many as one hundred estates probably existed between the coast to the east and Holkham and Swaffham to the west.

For the city dwellers an added attraction was the picturesque coastline with its resorts like Cromer and Yarmouth, and villages like Hunstanton, Sheringham and Mundesley. These, and others, often featured in paintings, with summer views on the sands of beached fishing boats and bathing huts, or with quaint street scenes and local people.

Turning now to one of the estates, and a well known family, brings John Crome on to the scene. Thomas Harvey lived at Catton Hall to the north of Norwich; he was a collector of fine paintings and an amateur artist. He introduced the then young John Crome to the works of English and Dutch masters, including Gainsborough and Hobbema, and encouraged him in his study of painting. Here he copied Gainsborough's 'Cottage Door'. Through Mr Harvey he was fortunate enough to meet William Beechey, a well known portrait painter, who later married a Norwich lady. Beechey seems to have offered much advice to John Crome who visited Beechey on numerous occasions, often spending time in his 'painting room' or dining with him in the evenings.

In another grand house close to Norwich lived the Gurney family – at Earlham Park. John Gurney, the banker, commissioned John Crome to teach his seven daughters lessons in drawing. It is said that from this time onwards Crome never looked back. After he had been a tutor for a few years, the Gurney family went on holiday, in 1802, on a tour of the Lake District, and invited John Crome along too. A year later he was to become involved in the setting up of the Norwich Society.

The fact that John Crome was later appointed art master at the Norwich Grammar School is of some interest. His son, John Berney, was head boy at the time, and two of his pupil friends were James Stark and George Vincent – all destined to become famous artists of the school. On the staff of the school was Charles Hodgson, the maths master, whose son David was later to feature prominently. Whether this association had much bearing on the early years of the school is unclear for both Stark and Vincent had already received tuition from John Crome before this appointment.

What does bring a pause for thought is the ease with which one artist must have met another within the confines of the old walled and compact city. It may have been fortunate, too, that Norwich did not grow rapidly, like other cities, though the population proceeded to more than double during the active life of the school, reaching 80,000 in the 1870s.

Over the years countless associations were to develop between the artists in Norwich and the people of Norfolk and beyond. This happy development allowed the school to promote itself with artists giving instruction far and wide and settling in places like Yarmouth, Kings Lynn, Cambridge and London. But from its very beginning the stability of Norwich, with its culture and pockets of wealth, stood to ensure the future of the Norwich School – this was no more so than with the founding of the Norwich Society of Artists in 1803.

THE NORWICH SOCIETY OF ARTISTS AND THE NORWICH EXHIBITIONS

There had long been a tradition of Societies in Norwich in the eighteenth century, the Norwich Botanical Society being an example of this. Towards the end of the century more visiting artists were being attracted to Norwich and, as a further sign of an interest in art becoming established, exhibitions began to be held. In 1796, the first year that James Sillett happened to exhibit at the Royal Academy in London, there was a show in Norwich of old master paintings and others by English, including local, artists. The mood, then, was becoming set for an art group to form a society too.

The Norwich Society of Artists had a membership of nearly eighty names during its thirty year history. The full members numbered fifty and the honorary ones twenty-nine. The honorary members could not be residents of Norwich; some were well known artists, like Sir William Beechey, who were associated with the Royal Academy in London, founded thirty-five years earlier. Others were artists like Thomas Churchyard, from Woodbridge, and Edwin Cooper from Beccles. It is possible that important members like Beechey, from outside Norfolk, helped the prestige of the society, which otherwise consisted of, it seems, local people, the full members.

Over the years the members came and went and, from small beginnings when the membership numbered around fifteen, it rose in the last five years to nearly fifty. Many of the members who exhibited have names which are more or less lost to memory. The founding members are of course well known but these, and others like Stark and Vincent, whose names are carried over to this day as Norwich School painters of some repute, number a mere twenty, if that.

Several Norwich artists, like the Stannard brothers, H Ladbrooke and SD Colkett, did not join the society, though they exhibited with it often enough. The painters of Norwich and around were thus brought together by being not only society members,

Mountain and River landscape. Watercolour.
SD Colkett, signed label on reverse
6 1/2 x 9 3/4 ins., 16.6 x 24.8 cms.
*A late style painting, circa 1860; Colkett by
then had 'modernised' his tree forms. He was
a persistent painter of sheep. Watercolours of
his appear from time to time.*

Wooded Parkland. Watercolour. **SD Colkett**
8 x 11 ins., 20.4 x 27.9 cms.
*The handling of the trees suggests Colkett,
who was never much of a figure painter, but
enjoyed using bright colours. Several of his
paintings show simple gateways mid-picture.
Many Norwich paintings were based on the
parks near Norwich like Earlham and
Kimberley, and Gunton to the north.*

FACING PAGE TOP
Barn, Evening. Oil on mahogany panel. **H Bright**
9 3/4 x 14 7/8 ins., 24.8 x 37.8 cms.
This sketchy oil shows Bright's interest in lighting effects. Another similar sized version exists with the three logs, like the cow, reflecting the sunset. Water is just visible in the foreground in both. Bituminous paint (Vandyke brown), often used by Norwich painters, tended to dry out and contract with age.

FACING PAGE BOTTOM
The Wensum near New Mills. Watercolour. **O Short**
Inscription on reverse
9 1/4 x 17 5/8 ins., 23.5 x 44.8 cms.
This is Obadiah's version of John Crome's famous 'Norwich River: Afternoon' (recently acquired by the Castle Museum). It seems John Thirtle may have done a version too, which Obadiah copied as Thirtle's typical initials appear to be on the end wall of a house – looking like supporting irons. Obadiah was not a figure painter and felt happier leaving the boat empty. Crome had a crew of five!

The Castle. Black chalk and body colour on stiff buff paper. **H Bright**, signed
7 1/8 x 5 1/8 ins., 18 x 13 cms.
The underlying colour of the paper shows through in this unusual castle composition. Bright enjoyed painting castles (e.g. Orford), and cows, and successfully combined his lighting effects in a later style painting. Another Norwich School display of flowers is seen in a corner.

but also society exhibitors. This point is important as collectively, linked together, they formed a group which became a school.

Once the painters began to establish themselves the scene was set for a society of art to expand. In all, the Norwich Society had some twenty-seven exhibitions which were well supported. In addition to these there were two memorial exhibitions, one for John Crome in 1821, and two loan ones. Ten exhibitions occurred before the society ran into trouble in 1815 and split up. The following year a breakaway group headed by Robert Ladbrooke, with John Thirtle, James Sillett and Joseph Stannard, Ladbrooke's pupil, and others held their own exhibition styled 'The Twelfth Exhibition of the Norfolk and Norwich Society of Artists'. It seems one cause of the rift may have been jealousy on the part of R Ladbrooke as he watched his old school friend, John Crome, painting better than him! Another reason may have been the wish to exclude amateurs. Henry Ladbrooke suggests that it was the expensive society suppers that his father did not approve of. However, the new society, exhibiting under an expanded title, could not compete with the original one and, after three years, they were reunited.

Robert Ladbrooke did not exhibit again with the old society until after Crome's death. There followed a two year gap in exhibitions from 1826 when the original venue was pulled down. Then the society changed its name to the Norfolk and Suffolk Institution for the Promotion of Fine Arts and moved its exhibitions to the new Corn Exchange. However, lack of money and the inability to sell many of its exhibits forced its demise. The drift away from Norwich and Norfolk by some artists, including John Sell Cotman, cannot have helped. It held its last exhibition in 1833 and also, that year, was involved in helping to handle Edwin Cooper's memorial exhibition.

There appears to have been a gap in exhibitions in Norwich for six years, but this did not deter the artists from continuing to send exhibits to London, to both the Royal Academy and the British Institution in particular. Then in 1839 the first exhibition of the Norfolk and Norwich Art Union was held. Differently titled exhibitions were held in 1840 and 1842 and, after a gap of a few years, the First Exhibition of the Norfolk and Norwich Association for the Promotion of Fine Arts was held in 1848. As Norwich's trade flourished again, so did the exhibitions. Perhaps there was a greater sense of well-being. These Association exhibitions ran for nine years before stopping for a while. JB Ladbrooke, who was quite an active artist at that time and produced a number of dated paintings confirming this, subscribed to six of these shows, on two occasions with a dozen paintings or so.

A mixture of exhibitions occurred over the next twenty years including five for 'modern artists' between 1860 and 1871, organised by the Association, to which the three Ladbrooke brothers all sent something. Then, as late as 1878, Obadiah Short and Maria Margitson,

FACING PAGE
Ell Hall. Watercolour. **JB Ladbrooke**, monogrammed
JBL, dated 1870
16 5/8 x 13 7/8 ins., 42.2 x 35.2 cms.
This is probably a house in the Peak District,
framed in Leeds following its commission. In later
life JB did an increasing number of upright
paintings showing tall trees and foliage with
highlights, mostly in oils but occasionally in
watercolour too. He was painting pictures of
Snowdon at this time and so it is possible he
passed this spot en route. He might even have
stayed at the hall!

JB Ladbrooke's niece, were exhibiting as 'living artists' at the Victoria Hall Gallery. Later that year there was a big loan exhibition to which a lot of Norwich School paintings were lent from private collections, to raise money for the St Peter Mancroft Church Restoration Fund. It seems pretty clear that after 1878 the artists themselves were not involved with any more local exhibitions.

Not only did the exhibition titles change, but so did the style of painting. This change can easily be seen by looking at the paintings of JB Ladbrooke, which span fifty years, and finish with a style recognisable as Victorian. When John Crome became involved with the Norwich Society in 1803 he was already thirty-five years old. It says much of the Norwich School that it was not until some seventy-five years later, and over half a century after Crome's death, that it virtually ceased to exhibit.

View of Snowdon. Watercolour. **JB Ladbrooke**
21 7/8 x 16 3/8 ins., 55.6 x 41.6 cms.
This late period watercolour is the same size as
another of his watercolours of the same subject
painted in 1871. He likewise painted Snowdon in
oils, dating the picture Feb. 26 1870. He has used
bodycolour for highlighting water, which now
stands out against the faded silver birches.

A View of Norwich. Oil on canvas. **JB Ladbrooke**
13 ¹/₂ x 17 ³/₄ ins., 34.3 x 45 cms.
*This painting is likely to date from much the
same time as his brother Henry's view of
'Norwich from Mousehold', 1823. The city is
dominated by Castle Mound and shows the castle
before it underwent alterations in 1834. Old
varnish obscures some detail but the red strips in
the sunset are found in other (early) JB paintings
illustrated. The view, under the influence of his
father who used dark pigments, has a Dutch look
endowed upon it by the formal portrayal of the
cows and sheep. Until recently the painting was
attributed to G Vincent; but a glance at the
foreground reveals JB's plant life! Furthermore, a
sort of preliminary drawing, with sheep, can be
found in his sketchbook in the V&A.*

Two
Landscapes

Wooded landscapes • Open landscapes
Hills and mountains • Rivers and seashores
Animal portraits in landscapes

PEOPLE PONDERING unknown Norwich School landscapes, particularly the oil paintings, will need to have certain concepts in mind, if they are to accept the notion that what they are viewing are indeed works of the school. The paintings need to be understood. If only it were so simple as to list the characteristics that apply to this school in contrast to others! Nevertheless certain clues appear with enough frequency for people with a knowledgeable interest to be able to comment with some confidence: 'These are Norwich School pictures.' So, taking a look at the chief categories of landscape painting may help to bring a better perspective to their understanding.

WOODED LANDSCAPES

Trees and woodlands, often divided by lanes and pathways, with a figure or two, were the artists' most popular subjects. Today, these are what the school is known for. The artists set out initially to paint the countryside around Norwich, so it is hardly surprising that the content of many paintings was chiefly trees with wayside cottages tucked amongst them. These cottages were often thatched, prettily gabled, with dew ponds close by. Ducks and other birds were commonly painted where there was water, and, if there was a figure, there was often a dog at its side. Nearby, horses or donkeys, and cows or sheep, were found in the open spaces. There was always an emphasis on animals as much of what was painted was composed of a farming community; their presence brought warmth to a picture. The varied figures on the lanes around Norwich were made up of pedlars and tinkers, whole families which may have been gypsies, or a shepherd with his boy and dog following a flock. Evening scenes sometimes showed a traveller returning home. The choice depended on the artist. James Stark liked gypsies, George Vincent painted pedlars, SD Colkett portrayed driven sheep and Anthony Sandys liked sunset scenes with a solitary traveller.

As often as not, these people were placed not in the immediate foreground, but at a safe distance, so that they did not intrude upon the main subject matter. At times they were added like a piece of embroidery to a part of the picture, like initials on a handkerchief. The artists took great care to paint their figures in a small and soft way. By and large the landscape painters were not portrait painters, and in this sense they differed from some of the mainstream English names who immediately preceded them. To make the point clearer, nor were they painters of people to the extent that George Morland often portrayed them – prominently with a landscape backdrop. The reverse was the case, and this is one of the significant aspects of the school, as the artists just wanted to paint the scenes for what they were. Some of them must have known that their figure-painting was clumsy at the best of times. It is worth mentioning that probably one out of every three landscapes in oil or watercolour was finished without a figure or an animal.

The Norwich School painters, par excellence, were tree painters. John Crome painted the Poringland oak, which hangs in the Tate Gallery. The ageing Winfarthing oak was a popular subject too. The variety of tree painting was of course tremendous and for this reason deserves consideration. Some of the early landscapes showed a Dutch influence; this in time mellowed into a softer 'Norwich' style, before lapsing into a Victorian one. In the main the roughly rounded mass of trees was a common choice for painters wanting an easier task at times, with the characteristic dabs of paint to represent the clumps of leaves and more purposeful touches to show the leaves

A Country Lane. Oil on millboard. **JB Ladbrooke**
9 x 10 7/8 ins., 22.8 x 27.6 cms.
*This is a middle period painting on a board
with a 'Roberson' indent and an Ackermann
label. The female figure walking up the lane
was disliked by an early owner and was
'rubbed' out (the ghost of her face is still just
discernible). The clouds are characteristic of
JB, so is the crosshatched grass and the
cluster of plants in the corner. There is a hole
in the bank, a foxes' earth; JB, with other
Norwich painters, used black paint effectively
from time to time.*

The Road to the Valley. Oil on millboard.
H Ladbrooke
12 x 14 ins., 30.5 x 35.5 cms.
*'Henry Ladbrook' is written on the back of
this Rowney & Co. millboard, together with
the name Stephen Abbott Esq., Castle Acre,
who once owned the picture. It is still in its
original Thirtle frame, dating the painting to
the late 1830s. The heavily detailed foliage,
and the vegetation stuck in a corner like a
stamp, confirm the artist's hand. This early
style is still classically Dutch. A larger
version, more overpoweringly wooded with a
dozen sheep and a shepherd, is probably the
main study – illustrated in Harold Day's
book. But, as so often happens, the smaller
picture is a more pleasing composition with
its yellow ochre foliage. The figure should be
noted for its colours.*

29

FACING PAGE
'Eaton Old Church from Keswick Mill'. Oil on oak panel. **J Stark** inscription on reverse
14 1/2 x 12 ins., 36.8 x 30.5 cms.
This picture reveals the transformation from Stark's tightly painted early Norwich period to the looser style of the 1830s, which eventually developed into the so-called Windsor one. There is plenty of colour with each tree being given its allotted variety, something Colkett (his pupil) tried to copy. Many of Stark's lanes show a herd of cows heading to a corner point – in a picture like this it is something of a signature.

themselves. James Stark's trees have been aptly likened to broccoli (A Hemingway) in his earlier Norwich years.

The size of a tree mass was often substantial in relation to the size of an oil painting. This allowed the artist to develop much of interest under and between the trees. Glimpses of cottages, seen mid-distance between tree trunks, their pale cream, sometimes yellow, plaster reflecting the light were frequently featured by James Stark, Crome's son William Henry and Alfred Stannard. On some occasions, in these wooded paintings, trees are found spanning the whole canvas, again a Stark feature, with the eye being led through the wood down a lane. This called for the use of colourful foliage, against the dark background, to lighten the painting and make it pleasing, not only justifying its use but also explaining it. This 'bright' idea grew into a habit and became a successful sign of Norwich School tree painting.

The denser complex masses were sometimes broken up within by the sharper profile of a tree, or two, with brighter colours, a willow or a massive oak for example, besides the clever use of light flowing between trunks and foliage. Many artists clearly identified their trees; there is no difficulty spotting George Vincent's beautifully portrayed oak trees, or those of JB Ladbrooke, and Vincent's willow trees, which are often crack willows. The successful painting of trees, in whatever form, was perhaps where their chief talents lay. The smooth appearance of a group of trees could be quickly shed to reveal the power that some artists had to portray trees in their finest form. Displaying the grandeur of oak trees with jagged branches and boles in their trunks – perhaps glowing with the softness of autumn colours with splashes of light here and there – marked the peak of their achievements. When the trees grew on golden sandy banks or paths, so often a Norfolk feature, their pictures finished up richer still. Without the ability to portray trees their wooded landscape painting would have been of little consequence. *The Norwich School will always be known for its trees and by its trees.*

It is worth studying some of the tree configurations as these reveal the trends of the artists. Some liked to pair their trees, often with contrasting colours and shapes to give variety; this is seen in examples of Colkett's work, in particular, with his simple or complicated pairs. Underneath the foliage umbrella the tree trunks take on different shapes. Colkett again used to give a twist or two to his more slender trunks, so that they sometimes curved gracefully upwards like raised elephants' trunks. One of the Norwich School fashions was to give the trunks a rather pleasing reflection of light as if they were clothed in sunlit lichens, sometimes green and sometimes silvery grey. This is clearly seen in James Stark's paintings, but, significantly, by the time his son, Arthur James, was well-established, as is seen in the painting illustrated, this effect for him at least had seen its day under the influence of the Victorians.

The charming characteristic of Norwich School trees rests with the paint touches, over the whole tree, whether loosely or deftly applied. Tree painting also allowed for the use of eye-catching colours; that is how the Norwich School painters understood matters. So they often created a bright and cheerful brilliance, which granted the natural foliage a more verdant life than it deserved, especially when sunlight had been borrowed from more than one source to acquire the effect! Anyone liking Norwich School landscapes should first study the trees for, where a leafy tree is to be found, its 'foliage print' will be more of a pointer than any other to the school. It is not impossible to learn how the artists painted their trees and how these varied during their lifetimes.

This opens the way to not only spotting a Norwich School painting, but also distinguishing, with luck, between artists, even if it means remembering a lot of different trees! In this respect, the method of painting, in oils, clumps of leaves, a striking feature of Norwich School (oak) trees, by grouping them into many fingers and thumbs of foliage at times, openly spread like a gloved hand, albeit three fingered, well illustrates the point – with JB Ladbrooke having been the keenest proponent of all. This technique, no doubt developed from John Crome's teaching, is well deployed in some of the Ladbrooke paintings here – pleasantly painted in golden browns and greens it could perhaps be referred to quite simply as the 'glove' effect.

All these features combined in one way or another form the essence of Norwich School tree painting.

OPEN LANDSCAPES

It is true to say that if the artists were not portraying wooded landscapes they were instead being challenged to paint colourful views in the wider open spaces of East Anglia. So it comes as no surprise to find one painting after another depicting heath-land, marshland, or a river valley like the Yare valley. The land being flat had many windmills so some artists chose to feature them. John Crome made famous the windmill on Mousehold Heath. Extending the example of his master, Anthony Sandys seems to have specialised in windmills, often against the background of a rich sky.

It was the sky in particular that fired many artists to concentrate on cloud formations. One of the best-known views in the Castle Museum is the painting by Henry Bright of ruined St Benedict's Abbey, under a brooding mass of storm clouds. The sky seems to command the canvas. Another is his view of a mill in the fens bathed in a sunset. This similarly successful large painting is composed of stunning bright lengths of sky. The lighting effects are the key to Bright's success. It is no wonder he had so many pupils when he was teaching in London! John Middleton, incidentally, was one of them – relishing heath scenes on the north Norfolk coast around Weybourne, a location he also shared with Bright.

Samuel David Colkett was just as at ease painting landscapes full of bright sky as he was with wooded lane scenes, where the colour rested with the trees. His most atmospheric skies were probably painted when he lived near the sea at Yarmouth, which he did for ten years. Using scenes along the Yare valley he could choose his time of day in which to portray them. Some with bright blue skies and few clouds were done when the sun was high, at other times he was looking west up the valley into an evening sky. Often his eye was taken to a distant horizon marked by a windmill or church tower. Sometimes he cleverly constructed his painting within a circle – just indeed as the real eye saw the landscape.

It has always been said that the light and the skies of East Anglia have something special to offer, and for that reason it is easy to understand how pleasing many of these open landscapes appear. Some heavily wooded views, on the other hand, are prone to criticism for being darkened by an over-powering tree mass; often ageing and dirty varnish contribute to their lack-lustre appearance. Furthermore, trying to clean such paintings is not always easy as the green colours, or what is sometimes left of them, can fly in the face of solvents. These fugitive pigments have caused many paintings to be touched up over the years so that the present day tree mass is not what the artist

The River Yare at Whitlingham.
Oil on canvas. **SD Colkett**
*14 1/2 x 18 3/4 ins.,
36.8 x 47.6 cms.
This painting, perhaps
dating to the 1830s, realises
something more of Colkett's
ambitions departing from his
better known lane scenes.
There is a classical look to
the piece; it was once
described as being 'style of
Varley'. The castle and
cathedral show on the
skyline. The curling sky is a
reminder of G Vincent. The
name of Capt. Alexander is
pencilled on the stretcher;
Dickes mentions him in
connection with restoration
work, something Colkett also
undertook. Alfred Stannard
painted a scene very similar,
the same river bend with
three men in a rowing boat,
in 1833.*

The Yare Valley. Oil on
mahogany panel. **SD Colkett**
*9 7/8 x 13 5/8 ins., 25 x 34.6 cms.
This painting, from a
Yarmouth source, was most
likely painted when he lived
there between 1843 and
1854. The trees, with gently
twisting branches (he altered
the low left branch to give it
a double twist), are good
examples of his style. The
valley is filled with light as
the sun rises in the east. His
freshness here is more
successful than the tightness
sometimes found in more
formal and early paintings,
under the influence of Stark.
Later, with his move from the
coast to Cambridge, his touch
became quite Victorian.*

33

contrived. This problem does not apply in quite the same way to open views where much more sky and brightness may predominate. These open landscapes may have been easier to paint, with few (if any) trees and plenty of sky, so, many artists may have found this type of landscape more to their liking.

Identifying such landscapes as works of the Norwich School can prove more difficult. There is often little or no foliage to rely on. Instead, the subject matter may reveal the location, especially if there is a wherry in sight or Norwich's cathedral spire is on the horizon. Otherwise, the fashionable bright colours, sandy lanes, and splashes of 'Crome's' light, perhaps on a windmill sail, may be enough of a clue.

HILLS AND MOUNTAINS

The painters did not confine themselves to Norfolk. As the school grew in stature, the artists took themselves further afield. Wales, Scotland, the Lake District and the Peak District were all visited. George Vincent is known for several fine views in the Scottish mountains and lochs. JB Ladbrooke likewise visited Loch Katrine and Loch Lomond, and further painted views in Wales, with Snowdon in the background, or just simply rocky streams in the hills. His brother Henry travelled to Yorkshire and the north of England; a large view of Bolton Abbey was painted as a result in 1841. Henry Bright produced colourful works from his trips to Wales, but for his real mountain scenes he is perhaps overlooked – on his visits to the Continent he produced magnificent views on the Rhine. Of the Crome family John Crome is said to have excelled himself with his large oil painting of the Slate Quarries in North Wales. His son, William Henry, also ventured into the mountains but without the same effect, although, like his father, he did place the occasional figure sitting or fishing at a rock's edge, but rather precariously. It says much of the artists that so many travelled; more than a third of the artists featured in this book visited mountain regions to paint.

RIVERS AND SEASHORES

The wherry and the windmill contributed much to the making of Norwich School paintings. The River Yare, meandering from Norwich to Yarmouth through water meadows at Whitlingham, past Postwick Grove and Surlingham and on to the flatter countryside between fields and marshes on its way to Yarmouth, gave rise to thousands of paintings. Anthony Sandys knew the river and valley only too well; he brought home views of boats on the Yare and drainage mills in the marshland. He often placed two or three horses in these tranquil settings, quietly grazing. He, and many others, found their chance in these scenes to put their carefully learnt skills into practice.

George Vincent's most attractive paintings have been of partly wooded country-side with water running by. Here, he often used a bank of trees as a backdrop, as in the famous Travelling Pedlar paintings. Vincent cleverly employed a central tree mass, and then painted different more distant views to either side. He liked to paint an oak or willow tree, sometimes a split crack willow, as his colourful centrepiece. He used pigments masterfully. Some claim he was Crome's most talented pupil – his richly coloured leaf-work, at times, glowingly dotted like polished emeralds on a jeweller's tray (Pevensey Bay). Vincent also sprinkled flowers in his foregrounds, just as if he had strewn gold dust for the same effect. George Vincent's ability to produce some of

Mountain Lake. Oil on canvas. **H Ladbrooke**
18 x 24 ins.,
45.7 x 61 cms.
This painting was one of a collection of three, the other two being views of Redmount, and Kettle Mills on the River Gaywood, Kings Lynn. Richard Wilson's 'View of Snowdon from Llyn Nantlle', now in the Castle Museum and Art Gallery, Nottingham, may have inspired Henry to produce this composition. Note Henry's pair of red figures. The tree foliage can be compared with that of the slender pair of trees in HL's 'Nr Falmouth', which is all about trees! The set of three, judging from their style, would have been painted in the 1860s when he lived at Kings Lynn.

Loch Katrine. Watercolour on paper board.
JB Ladbrooke
9 1/4 x 13 ins.,
23.5 x 33 cms.
This view, showing Ben Venue towering over the Loch and Ellen's Isle, was also the subject of a larger oil painting by JBL. In 1848 he exhibited a view of Loch Lomond; it is likely he visited Katrine, close by, on the same visit to Scotland to study this view (in an early Boswell frame to support a similar date).

the best pictures in the Norwich School rests with his creation of fine compositions and use of colour. The formula of producing a landscape featuring water, trees on a bank beyond, and distant views has probably been the most successful of all complex Norwich School paintings. The Pedlar painting is one of such masterpieces, especially worth studying in the Castle Museum alongside Pevensey Bay.

Many of the artists travelled to the coast. Thomas Lound liked to catch the morning light, for it cast long reflections on the wet beach amongst the fisher folk, especially in the winter when the sun shone low. The influence of the famous painter, Bonington, is quite apparent. Alfred Priest, on the other hand, reveals a Cotman touch; Priest painted beach scenes in summertime looking up the coast, with the sun shining back from the brilliant faces of wet pebbles sparkling brightly – the gemstones of the seashore.

Meg. Pencil, pen and watercolour. **E Cooper**
7 x 4 1/8 ins., 17.8 x 10.5 cms. (sight)
'Richard Ward's favourite dog Meg, by Edwin Cooper of Beccles' is pencilled on the reverse of the drawing. She lived at Salhouse Hall, close to the Broads, with her master.

Yarmouth brought other painters to its beaches and river mouth. John Crome painted Yarmouth jetty. His son John Berney painted the famous Yarmouth Water Frolic, part of the Iveagh Bequest. George Vincent made a large painting of the Dutch fair on Yarmouth beach, not long after Nelson's Column was completed. Here, this monument stands back from the sea with a crowd of more than one hundred and fifty people between it and the shoreline – making it a busy picture. The Stannard family, who often painted ships at sea, used the sands for their subjects too.

Delightful paintings of fishermen, with their boats and haul, provide us with a lasting record of the life and work these men endured. In fact, much of Norwich School landscape painting is memorable for its historic portrayal of the life and times of this part of eastern England and the toils of the past.

ANIMAL PORTRAITS IN LANDSCAPES

The Norwich School painters loved their animals and not infrequently some of them produced portraits of animals in landscape settings. This was particularly true of Edwin Cooper who spent most of his life painting horses, dogs and even prize bulls. George Vincent, perhaps, took his cue from Cooper when he painted a close-up of two cows resting in a meadow under a tree. Another horse painter was CJW Winter

Fishing Smack on Yarmouth Beach. Oil on Roberson board. **T Lound**
6 ¹/₂ x 10 ins., 16.6 x 25.4 cms.
A watercolour study of this subject is in the Reeve Collection at the British Museum. The oil, painted on a Roberson board from Long Acre, London, shows fishermen landing their catch on a winter's morning; the sun lies low in the south-east and is reflected in the wet sand as the tide goes out. Another picture in the BM in crayon is dated Dec 36, showing his interest in winter sketching. The clouds and their colours are clues to his work.

Beach scene. Watercolour on Whatman paper.
A Priest, signed and dated 1846
9 x 13 ins., 22.9 x 33 cms.
Boats beached on the sand after the storm. The shore is scattered with shimmering stones before the tide line. The crystal clear focus of light on the clouds, rounded as they are, shows Priest was successfully influenced by JS Cotman. Bodycolour, opaque watercolour, is used for the breaking waves. The price of the picture 150 years ago was four guineas.

who probably accepted commissions to paint somebody's favourite animal. Anthony Sandys made drawings of chickens and sheep on his tour of the Lake District. AJ Stark made a number of horse studies and, as mentioned elsewhere, his father recorded his own dog 'Trim'. John Paul was a horse painter too, a signed portrait of a grey seeming to show an individual style.

It was fun to visit one house with a collection of Norwich School landscapes, whilst photographing material for this book, and to find a pair of Norwich Terriers on guard duty. They lived many miles from Norwich and, of course, had no idea that they were protecting a few paintings of that distant location. Like the pinnacles of Norwich Cathedral tower the Norwich Terriers' ears point skyward, acting as small antennae. This made the dogs look very alert for the occasion!

Huntsman and Hounds. Oil on metal.
E Cooper, signed
6 1/4 x 8 1/2 ins., 15.9 x 21.6 cms.
A pair of hounds are seen stalking their quarry in the undergrowth; a little above the pheasant Cooper has hidden his name amongst the blades in black. The reverse of the sheet shows a pencil plan of the subject, with directions for this painting, which he nearly obeyed – there are three hounds!

Waterfall in Scotland. Oil on mahogany panel.
G Vincent, monogrammed and dated 1831
10 x 12 ins., 25.4 x 30.5 cms.
Vincent painted a scene in Glen Shira, Inveraray,
in 1824, probably from memory. A letter he wrote
in the Fleet Prison in December of that year
suggests he had just completed it. In the mid-
distance a split waterfall is clearly visible, very
similar to this one, with much the same
surroundings. He also did three versions of the
illustrated picture, all with variations, which
suggests this subject was his own composition –
based on his original painting of 1824, perhaps.
It is worth noting his very detailed foliage and his
late style sky in one of his last recorded paintings.
Probably his finishing touches were first the
fishing rod then GV 1831 – both are coloured the
same. Patrick Nasmyth's works are sometimes
confused with Vincent's – they painted in the
same Scottish locations, including Inveraray.

Anglers by a Mountain Stream. Oil on oak panel.
WH Crome
7 1/4 x 9 5/8 ins., 18.4 x 24.3 cms.
A slight figure, in red and white, perched on a rock is a WHC 'signature'. This green mountain scene probably dates to his mid period. He was living at Liverpool in 1839 and Edinburgh in 1846, exhibiting both there and at Manchester in the 1840s. This picture is instructive for its colouring.

Norwich. Watercolour. **T Lound**
4 7/8 x 7 1/4 ins., 12.4 x 18.3 cms.
The city from the NW. showing some of the old churches, one with a spire, St. Gregory's - the cathedral is out of sight. Another view, from the Wensum Meadows, is in the remarkable Castle collection of small watercolours by Lound.

Three
Two artists

JB Ladbrooke and A Sandys

OVERLEAF
Figure on a Lane. Pencil drawing. **JB Ladbrooke**
Illustration from sketchbook. (ref. E907–1928)
5 3/4 x 9 3/8 ins., 14.6 x 23.8 cms.
Reproduced with photograph kindly supplied by the Victoria & Albert Museum

FACING PAGE
A Romantic Evening. Oil on Rowney & Foster millboard. **JB Ladbrooke**
13 x 17 ins., 33 x 43.2 cms.
This unsigned and untitled painting was probably done a while before 1830, and then displayed in one of his brother Robert's frames. The study was repeated a little later with cows instead of people, and again in 1856 with a cathedral spire in the distance. All of this suggests the pictures are compositions, as many of his paintings are. (Interestingly, Dickes illustrates similar subject matter, painted by his father, with trees and lake facing the other way.) The orange-red sunset appears in some of his early work though the lighting effect on the trees, produced with a golden glaze, is special. A sunken punt adds to the dreaminess of a summer's evening. A little red flower can be spotted in the shadows.

THE STUDY of any style of painting, let alone the Norwich School, can provoke a depth of interest that becomes time-absorbing. No apology is therefore made for concentrating on two artists who show a different response to the influence of Crome. It is only by careful study of particular artists that much more can be revealed about the habits of the whole school. The text has been selective for this very reason, rather than choosing to dash through a list of several artists with little mention of each.

John Berney Ladbrooke and Anthony Sandys have been chosen as the two artists. They will be discussed in a general way, with the next chapter focusing on the detail found in their works. Their choice happens for a variety of reasons. It has already been said that much has been written on first generation artists, those born late in the eighteenth century like Crome and Cotman. Many illustrations are available, too, of the works of these two artists, and others like Thirtle, Stark and Vincent. However, the second generation artists, meaning John Crome's son, William Henry, and his contemporaries, have to some extent been neglected. The reason for this is obvious in that some of their works are not held in such high esteem, and lack of research has meant a failure in identifying, from an array of Norwich School paintings, the numbers available for study. There have, however, been excellent publications on Henry Bright, the Joy brothers from Yarmouth in a short article, and a brief resumé of the life of JB Ladbrooke to mark the centenary of his death, these being quite apart from general book studies of the Norwich School. So, by turning to two representatives of the second generation, and in particular their paintings, it is possible to shed more light on the School in its middle and later years.

This should be of interest because it is this form of painting which more often alights on the market due to its relative abundance, rather than the rarer works of Crome, Cotman, Vincent and Joseph Stannard and others of the first generation, many of which are in museums or private collections. By selecting this pair it is possible to show two quite different styles, each with the full flavour of the Norwich School. These two artists were born only three years apart and enjoyed a lengthy lifetime, living to beyond seventy. One of them, Ladbrooke, was a native of the city, the other was born in the north Norfolk countryside, at Hindringham, and later settled in Norwich. Both produced paintings derived from the countryside around Norwich, with JB Ladbrooke specialising in wooded landscapes and A Sandys in open landscapes. Only JB Ladbrooke of the two became a member of the Norwich Society of Artists (1828). Like many artists of the School they travelled far in the British Isles and both went to the Lake District and Scotland at different times. From these trips Ladbrooke produced many oil paintings and some watercolours; Sandys brought home sketch books of pencil drawings. Their way as artists began with a difference; A Sandys was known as a portrait painter before he took to landscapes in the 1840s; Ladbrooke, as if not to be outdone, did experiment in portrait painting too. However by the middle of the century both their styles were set in landscapes.

JOHN BERNEY LADBROOKE 1803–1879

This artist was born the third son of Robert Ladbrooke. His mother was formerly Mary Berney whose sister had married John Crome. His father taught him to draw and, at the age of thirteen, he exhibited for the first time in Norwich – a pencil sketch. He is then said to have studied a year with John Crome, just as his elder brother Henry had done.

There is a sketchbook in the Victoria and Albert Museum which belonged to JB Ladbrooke presumably around this time. It contains over forty sheets of Whatman paper, watermarked 1801, enclosed by marbled boards with calf back and corners and a brass clasp. He wrote his name clearly and boldly across the inside cover. It would appear from its contents that it might have been an exercise book used in drawing instruction. Of greatest interest are the nine monochrome watercolour sketches, one of which reveals his early interest in a linear approach to foliage detail (seen much in his late oils) pencilling in clumps of leaves using small groups of straight lines. Another shows a gabled house on the outskirts of Norwich beneath Mousehold Heath. There is also a panoramic pencil drawing of Norwich from a hill on the south east. This clearly shows the cathedral and a few churches, buildings along the river's edge and wherries on a bend in the river, with Mousehold Heath and its windmills beyond.

JB Ladbrooke once had in his possession a black and white Crome picture of palings and trees by a pond. This watercolour is in the Reeve Collection in the British Museum and is illustrated in the Crome book by the Cliffords. An inscription on its mount reads: 'Old Crome from his nephew JB Ladbrooke to J Norgate'. It is significant that the content of the first drawing in this sketch book is far from being dissimilar. Did his uncle, John Crome, give it to him for study purposes? Later, probably in his twenties, he incorporated similar palings in a small oil sketch firmly inscribing his name on the reverse as if to say: I've learnt how to do it!

In the 1820s his father set out to draw all the churches of Norfolk, some six hundred and sixty-seven. John Berney helped him with this task and later produced some of the lithographs. He seems to have visited London in the early 1820s when he twice exhibited at the Royal Academy. About the same time he followed his elder brother's example in giving drawing lessons styling himself as 'drawing master'. During the 1830s, he visited towns within reach of Norwich to give tuition, one of these places being Bungay; in the Castle Museum collection there are several drawings of scenes in that area. The most accomplished of his pupils was John Middleton, who sadly died young; another was WPB Freeman.

As is usual among artists the style of his painting varied considerably and this applies to both oils and watercolours. The cover plate, before 1830, shows a pattern

Facing page
The Footbridge. Watercolour. **JB Ladbrooke**
12 1/2 x 17 1/8 ins., 31.7 x 43.5 cms.
This finely painted watercolour has been attributed to JBL (Alec Cotman in 1972). JB did more watercolours than is generally realised. Many features suggest that this is his work too, amongst them the bank with black shadows. A similar little dog, with its paw raised, appears in another of his paintings, as does the wooden footbridge. The detail would make this a mid-period composition, once again concentrating on an oak tree, probably based on one of Stark's river scenes. JB frequently used gum arabic to bring out the darkest parts of a watercolour.

very different to his later oils. This particular subject is interesting for the fact that it has appeared in two other later guises by him. There is a bigger version with cattle in place of the figures and a later version still, dated 1856, which is a small oil showing a cathedral spire in the distance, quite freely painted. Subjects he liked were often repeated in this way. JB Ladbrooke was as much at ease painting large scenes as he was small ones. What is more, he seems to have enjoyed painting similar subjects in different sizes. He also varied his technique when painting on a smaller scale, either by making a sketch, or by deliberately rendering fine detail as though he were painting a large picture in miniature, as indeed he may have been requested to do.

Until recently it had not been widely appreciated that JB Ladbrooke was a watercolour artist of some standing. The late Alec Cotman, adviser to the Art Department of the Norwich Castle Museum, confidently pronounced the wooded river scene illustrated as the work of John Berney. This was at a time when little was known of his watercolour work; but, as it bears no signature, it has been difficult to prove Alec Cotman right, or wrong for that matter. When it turned up in East Anglia it had long lost its pedigree, once attached with sealing wax to the back of the paper. A little faded it still has glowing colours and a composition typical of what JB was best at. In a slightly different style, and with no doubt about its authenticity, is his view of Loch Katrine. There is a big oil version of this subject signed and indistinctly dated in the 1840s. As he exhibited a view of Loch Lomond in 1848 it is likely to date from much the same time, like the watercolour, which still has its birth certificate in the form of a contemporay Boswell-labelled frame backing.

Although JB, as he is often referred to, travelled to various parts of the British Isles painting views of waterfalls and mountains, like Snowdon in oils and watercolours, he was most at home in his native Norfolk painting the scenes he lived amongst and which, it seems, were dear to his heart. Some artists could excel with mountain scenes but, with JB, there is much more warmth in his smaller landscapes closer to Norwich. A chapter is devoted to a collection of half a dozen of such pictures, painted when he was probably at the height of his career. These typify what he was best at and what the Norwich School most stood for. He was without doubt a significant painter of the school and, to gain a proper insight into his capabilities, it is worth visiting the Castle Museum to see the lovely wooded landscape painting of 1864, 'Water Lane, Autumn'. This measures 30 inches by 40 inches – giving him all the space he needed to paint his oak trees with detail and colour. The painting is also well enough thought of to have been illustrated in three publications in the last thirty years!

Before leaving JB Ladbrooke it is worth mentioning his family. His father concentrated on landscape painting and employed a rather austere classical style in some of his earlier work, with brown the chief pigment. As these works are somewhat uninteresting many may not have survived in the same way that his son's paintings have done. Indeed, there are tales of some old paintings (not his) being used to serve up stirrup-cup, when trays were short; a dull picture might have had a spirited death, admired for quite the wrong reason! However, Robert's apparent later style is so different from his early work that it begs the question whether his eldest son, also Robert, painted a few landscapes, besides managing his own framing business. He is not known to have been an artist, but two R Ladbrooke signed oils have appeared in a very green vein more akin to the work of H Ladbrooke. As a professional picture framer he might have been at least familiar with managing oil paints.

In just the same way it was not revealed, until JB's sketchbook was examined, that JB himself was a dab hand at picture restoration – for want of anywhere else to record the fact, he had pencilled inside the back cover the dozen or so jobs he had carried out for a couple of customers. He listed the work of lining, cleaning and repairing various pictures like '2 pictures of Gods and Godifses (sic)' and repairing 'holes in the Bullrushes' – with his charges carefully summed up. Five shillings was the cost of 'lining Hed Vandyke' (sic).

Turning to Henry Ladbrooke it is hardly surprising to note that he came under his father's spell in his early years. Both painted similar panoramic views of Norwich with black clouds overhead, but Henry lightened his important view from Mousehold with plenty of green. His early style shows an unmistakable classical look, particularly in his broader landscapes, whereas his wooded scenes show a Dutch influence. These effects evaporated eventually, and by the 1850s his paintings had a very English look about them with some of the smaller ones having a delightful charm. Henry and his brother JB often chose the same subjects. Perhaps they travelled to the same places or copied one another, or used a Crome subject which they both knew, as seems to have occurred. A view of a lane near Shernbourne is one example. JB Ladbrooke painted his version in 1850, which gained the title 'Near Shambourne', a corruption of the proper name. Shortly after JB's version came to light, Henry's appeared too – this occurred some twenty-five years ago when many Norwich School paintings entered the art market as a new vogue of interest in the School developed. Which picture came first is not known, but Henry lived at Kings Lynn later in his life and was exhibiting views of other places near Lynn from 1848 onwards.

The other brother Frederick exhibits the same family style of painting, but, with few landscape works available for study, relatively little is known about him. Frederick lived at Bury St Edmunds; perhaps Henry visited him there as he painted at least one or two views of the town, with one of his larger more splendid paintings bearing the title, 'The Abbot's Bridge, Bury St Edmunds'.

In 1859 JB Ladbrooke bought a plot of land on Mousehold Heath on which he built a house and studio overlooking the city. The house was named after Robert Kett and called Kett's Castle Villa. In 1549 this gentleman and his followers had used the heath – it was wooded then, the name is derived from Moche Holt: great wood – as the site of their stronghold when marching against the city. This they did as a protest against the enclosure of commons, and for months they kept up their hostilities until defeated. However, for John Berney, this part of Mousehold eventually became a place of peaceful retirement.

ANTHONY SANDYS 1806–1883

The Norwich School had several portrait painters who furthered the tradition that ran before them. When Anthony Sandys began painting he chose to fill his canvases with the heads and shoulders of local people, exhibiting for the first time in Norwich in 1830. He continued to show portraits from time to time for the next thirty years. The first definite indication of a change in direction to landscape painting is provided by his inscription on the back of the 'Mill on Mousehold' canvas showing a date of 1848. Interestingly, at this time, his name was spelt 'Sands', as the plaque on the front of this painting shows. It was about 1855 that he changed his name to 'Sandys'. By the time of this picture he was obviously an accomplished landscape artist.

His early association with Norwich seems to have been as a textile dyer working for the firm of Stark and Mills. He was a journeyman. It was later that he became an artist and drawing master. Whereas JB Ladbrooke's claim to fame was to have an uncle called John Crome, Anthony's claim was to have a son called Antonio Frederick Augustus Sandys, born in Norwich in 1829. He became one of the Pre-Raphaelite group of painters and an artist of much greater merit than his father. There was also a daughter called Emma who, like her brother and father, became a portrait painter.

One of the great attractions of Anthony Sandys' paintings is his use of light, which of course came from falling under the influence of Crome. Sandys evolved his own style in this respect and, using exaggerated colour, was able to produce characteristically rich views of rural Norfolk. No paintings have turned up of scenes outside East Anglia though he travelled far from Norfolk sketching in pencil.

His tours took him to the Lake District in the summer of 1858. He sketched at Windermere, this included a picture of himself in bed one morning – carefully timed at half past seven. He visited Keswick, and Grange where he did a dozen tiny portraits of fowls and one of a pet lamb, besides views in the neighbouring countryside. Four years later he made off to Derbyshire with his sketchbook again, visiting Castleton and drawing many street scenes, one of which records the Royal Mail coach parked near the Nags Head, the inn where he was presumably staying. He did many sketches in the Peak District and more after moving on to Scotland. Some of these are inscribed with the place name, his initials, and dated to the day. It includes one done at the top of Ben Nevis; at the bottom of this sketch he mentions that it is a region of perpetual snow –

OVERLEAF PAGE 54
The Norwich River. Oil on oak panel. **A Sandys**, initialled and dated 1860
11 3/8 x 16 ins., 28.9 x 40.6 cms.
This colourful painting marks the best in Anthony Sandys' work. He did several views relating to the Whitlingham stretch of the river and probably exhibited this particular one in 1860. Fishing must have been a common pastime! Trowse Marsh lies ahead and Thorpe Marsh on the right bank, 'his' rowing boat on the left perhaps.

'Castleton'. Pencil Drawing. **A Sandys**
4 3/8 x 7 ins., 11.1 x 17.7 cms.
On the approach, early September 1862, and on the way to Scotland too. In 1858 he also toured the Lake District in summertime, sketching as he went.

dating it 'Sept, 10, 62'. When he was near Fort William he found a bothy with an old barrel for a chimney and, amusingly, brought a picture of that home too. His sketches are the holiday snaps of today.

When it came to oil painting it seems that he devoted his attention to views close to Norwich, often along the River Yare. In 1859 he is recorded as living on St Giles Hill. From the centre of Norwich he could easily have walked to Whitlingham Lane, which he painted more than once, and back, having spent the day sketching. Like other artists, he would have produced most of his formal paintings in his studio. The view on the River Yare, next to that very lane, was painted the following year 1860. In that year he exhibited two river scenes, one of which was known as 'A scene on the Norwich River' with a label asking six pounds, the other was 'A scene on the Back River' with a tag of five pounds. The Norwich River scene is almost certainly the painting illustrated in this book; the colourful other view, which was last seen when it appeared twenty-five years ago out of a private collection, is probably its delightful companion piece. Both bear identical monograms and dates.

He loved to paint windmills in his landscape settings and horses on the marshes, besides his river views with small sailing craft and wherries. For lighting effects he either used a midday sun or the glorious colours of an evening sky, as in his lane scene at Whitlingham. He appears to be at his best painting on a smaller scale rather than a larger one; the composition and interest of some of his bigger pictures are disappointing. He must have realised this as there are no records of any large pictures being painted. It is evident he often chose real scenes, whereas many of JB Ladbrooke's are imaginary. His paintings, too, show life with interest and sometimes a charming effect. The painting of horses on the marsh, munching hay in the midday sun, evokes just such a comment.

It seemed fitting to give prominence to his painting, inspired by John Crome, of a highlighted view on Mousehold – a windmill with its sails caught by the lingering rays of sun, and Norwich dying in distant shadow. This painting, at Stone Hills, held his attention some one hundred and fifty years ago, on an autumn evening. He carefully chose his colours and crowned the city with a spectacular sky cradling the castle, cathedral and churches beneath, their soft silhouettes showing on the skyline. He would have later trod the same road home, his picture completed and his own day's work well done, following the traveller he had just painted. He might even have been recording one of his own past journeys!

An Afternoon Stroll. Oil on Ackermann millboard.
A Sandys
10 x 12 ins., 25.4 x 30.5 cms.
*The title is pencilled on the reverse. It is not
surprising the painting was mistaken for one by
H Bright, whom Sandys studied, but the figure is
very much a Sandys type and so is the foreground
colouring in rich brown. Note the weatherboards
on the back of the store. A label on the reverse of
the frame shows the painting changed hands for
two guineas at the Sullivan Sale, Norwich, 1923.*

Drainage Mill. Oil on Winsor & Newton millboard. **A Sandys**
8 x 12 ins., 20.3 x 30.5 cms.
*This is the latest recorded painting by Sandys, done from 1878
onwards (W&N label type). The red ground colour of the board,
where little or no paint covers his pencil sketch of the wherry
and river banks, has been used to good effect. It was painted a
full seventy-five years after the founding of the Norwich Society.*

Four
Looking at detail

The Ladbrooke brothers and Anthony Sandys

View at Colney *(detail)*. Oil on millboard. **H Ladbrooke**
14 x 12 ins., 35.5 x 30.5 cms.
The low branch of the oak tree in the foreground is utterly characteristic of Henry –
zig-zagged into segments (tipped sideways it looks like a hedgehog).

The Cottage Children *(detail)*. Oil on oak panel. **JB Ladbrooke**, c.1835.
22 x 19 ins., 56 x 48.3 cms.
There is no better example of a distinctive foliage painter than JB Ladbrooke in the
whole Norwich School.

THERE IS no better way to learn about artists' habits than by studying the finer points exhibited in their works. This will complement what has already been learnt from simply gazing at a composition to gain an overall impression. By doing this the many characteristics of each artist can be appreciated and learnt and a store of knowledge built up. This is particularly important in the case of the Norwich School, as so many of their 'trees' look alike at first glance. Only by studying a fair number of paintings can this learning occur and, once done, some of it may hopefully be remembered. In order to illustrate these points and find out more about JB Ladbrooke, whose work is prominently illustrated, it is very necessary to turn to his brother Henry. The works of the two brothers are sometimes confused with one another and with other painters. Their half brother Frederick needs to be glanced at, but his works are rare.

The three Ladbrooke brothers were, above all, specialist tree painters. The study of their trees, therefore, affords the best opportunity to glean a few of their ways. It has been said of Henry Ladbrooke that he was the most dedicated tree painter of the school, producing the most detailed foliage. Certainly leaf work in some of his larger pictures receives extensive attention but, interestingly, for small fine detail it is worth looking at the foliage George Vincent could brush, well illustrated here in his waterfall painting. It is useful to study closely the foliage in Henry Ladbrooke's paintings, as the variety shown by the six spans nearly as many decades, from the 1820s onwards. A magnifying glass may come in handy. He died in November 1869, shortly after completing and exhibiting a large canvas entitled 'Near Falmouth'. This, and the largest painting in the book, a view of Norwich in 1823, show so clearly a change in style, which can be all too confusing. This great Norwich canvas was, until recently, attributed jointly to John Crome and his son John Berney. However some clever research (Norma Watt) revealed the true identity of the artist!

When it comes to sorting out the two important Ladbrooke brothers it quickly becomes apparent there are subtle differences to detect. In the descriptive analysis beneath some of Henry's paintings there is a reference to the zigzag pattern of low leafy branchwork that was so typical of him. Time and again paintings appear showing this feature, which is quite distinct from the bare branch-twig effect used by his brother JB, and from any one else for that matter. Since some of Henry's trees are busier than JB's there is a greater concentration in places of the finger-glove effect in the foliage, referred to earlier. Some of this is perhaps not quite as spiky as JB's; short fingers rather than long ones. The colouring, too, is a little different, and so is the highlighting on the tree trunks. Henry was so used to using green paint that even his sheep in the distance were often marked by a green blob, rather than a dirty white one.

Both Henry and his brother JB liked to put a small cluster of vegetation at the bottom of their paintings. Henry tended to pursue 'flower arranging' techniques when he did this, producing quite a display of full green leaf – certainly more than his brother liked to do. They were almost signing their paintings by doing this. Other artists introduced these leaf clusters, with a difference, particularly George Vincent and JB Crome who copied him.

Another interesting feature which Henry employed, when he had the space and purpose to do so, was the placing of two figures fairly close together, yet apart, but jointly engaged in the same activity. He often used red paint for their tunics, one perhaps sitting or standing, the other stooping or bending. One might be holding a

FACING PAGE

A View near Falmouth. Oil on canvas. **H Ladbrooke**
40 x 50 ins., 101.6 x 127 cms.
Henry painted this view from a sketch, a fact which must have applied to many of the Norwich paintings, done by the Rev. JA Ladbrooke. The owner of the painting believes the Reverend was a cousin; Henry himself was destined for the Church but became a painter instead. The zig-zag branch, the red tunics and the cloud fingers are some of his characteristics – retained to the end. Dickes illustrated this important picture. The price originally asked at exhibition in 1869 was fifty guineas. Red and blue are colours he repeatedly used for solitary figures.

rod, engaged in fishing, a pole, or a crook if a shepherd. JB Ladbrooke's figure painting was somewhat different. Two paintings illustrated show just such a pair of Henry's figures, which is also the case in his view of Bolton Abbey in the Castle Museum.

Henry's paintings are full of detail to learn – from the display of grey sky over the 'Mountain' and the 'Norwich' views to his familiar log painting in both of them. Not forgetting there were birches around, one or two of the logs look as though they might have been wrapped in nineteenth century silver foil which has started to peel away with time!

The many illustrations of JB Ladbrooke's paintings allow an even greater opportunity to tree gaze, from one of the earliest landscapes recorded by him to one of the latest. Without doubt JB was a very careful and accomplished tree painter, probably exceeding his brother Henry in capability. But Henry's softness of style was not always matched. JB tended to use more exciting colours, often in contrast. This was so in his bigger paintings when he was adding an autumnal glow to his foliage, a point which makes JB's paintings distinguishable from his brother's and other painters'. Dickes, in 1905, described his palette as 'rich and varied', although Henry, as well, could produce foliage with a polished amber-like look. Perhaps the most revealing painting in the book, the cover picture, though it is not large, clearly shows the effect of light from the sunset by the clever use of golden glazes on the tree trunks. On balance JB was able to achieve finer compositions than his brother – he was much more influenced by John Crome – and for this reason his tree painting often shows better, though Henry could run him a close second.

Looking more closely at JB's trees a curious feature is sometimes found amidst the foliage where, high up in the trees, as if the sky is peeping through the leaves, he has daubed splashes of blue here and there, often a much deeper hue than the sky beyond. Perhaps he felt the rays of light could not properly penetrate the treetops and were darkened in the process, but, whatever else he exactly meant, will never be known. When it does occur, this motif is found in his early to mid period works. Perhaps it is worth looking up into a tree in high summer to look for these shafts of blue light to see if an optical illusion is created when an intense blue is all around. Henry copied him only once or twice by placing a few dabs of 'blue', easily missed, in his tree tops. On one occasion he used the same colour as in his distant turquoise countryside – possibly for that very reason he, like his brother, felt the colours were not out of place dropped into the trees too!

Lastly, the two early views of Norwich by the Ladbrooke brothers are worth studying. What is immediately apparent is the steel-like coldness of part of Henry's work compared to the fire-like glow of JB's version. The different colours of the castle are worth comparing, for they portray this feeling. When Henry painted cottage scenes he often loved to show their chimney pots with smoke flowing away, flat in the wind; not so JB Ladbrooke. These views of Norwich, with its houses, reveal their differences in this respect too!

Frederick Ladbrooke was probably an artist as competent as JB, but it is difficult to draw many comparisons or distinctions as there is only a little material to study. The best of this is the small collection of paintings which came to the Castle Museum via the Spanton bequest. Originally Mr Spanton, of Abbey Gate St., Bury St Edmunds, framed Frederick's paintings for him. A descendant of the family passed these paintings on with a cast iron provenance. Two paintings of his are illustrated and,

happily, both are quite different. Each however shows the distant view held by very soft colours. The foreground of the busy picture, with two cows and a cowgirl, is reminiscent of JB Ladbrooke with the grass crisscrossed on the bank. The other painting, again with a brown and white cow but with a man following, is sketchy but revealing. It is another version of one of the Spanton bequest paintings. The illustrations are useful because, by their tree-painting styles, they show two distinct types, both of which are different from that of JB's to whom Frederick is closest in style. Just as interesting is the fact that JB also did a version of the sketchy picture, an elaborate painting with a female figure instead of cattle and drover. It seems the brothers could not get away from one another when it came to selecting a choice of scenes, or indeed styles.

So many Norwich School paintings are unsigned that it becomes a necessity to search for clues of authorship. About one third of JB Ladbrooke's paintings are made easy and are signed with initials, monogram or in full. Less often he added a date. Some earlier and mid period works contain a full 'JB Ladbrooke' signature, with a date in the mid to late period especially. Two paintings, dated in the 1850s, show a light coloured signature on a dark background. One early painting, of a tree and a ruin, revealed a full signature in dark paint in a dirty corner without an 'e'. This was how his brother, Robert, spelt his surname at the time. However, when signing with initials, he used black, dark brown, or red paint. The red appears in early and late works. Many of his smaller paintings contain no signature, and it appears it may have been a trick on occasions to place a splash of red, often tiny, somewhere close to where a signature might have appeared – dashed in like a flower in a dark corner. The cover picture shows just such a tiny display.

Of his brothers Henry signed his work less often. Bolton Abbey is fully signed and dated 1841, but this is a rarity. Occasionally he used initials, or a monogram as the pastiche reveals here. Frederick's few known landscapes all appear to be unsigned. A drawing of his however is recorded which bears his full name: Frederick Bagge Ladbrooke.

Since JB Ladbrooke was a painter who liked detail there is much else to observe in his work. In his foreground he often crosshatched his grass and in his skies he fingered his clouds too. Amongst his foliage he twigged his oak trees – all in a manner peculiar to him. There is much else besides – the number of sheep he liked to paint, not five, not three, but usually four, in his set pieces!

ANTHONY SANDYS

Anthony Sandys allows his detail to be appreciated in a totally different way. He has a brightness about some of his paintings that appears to be their striking feature. He used highlights carefully placed on windmill sails, and on fences and figures to emphasise and outline their shapes. He chose brilliant colours and like JJ Cotman, who was painting at the same time, was one of the most extravagant users of colour in the Norwich School.

He loved windmills and wherries, and, just as trees are used to study the Ladbrookes so windmills can be used for A Sandys. The windmill landscapes illustrated span four decades. Two of them are worth looking at closely as they both show the same windmill and cottage configuration. More remarkable is the grain store standing

FACING PAGE
Whitlingham Lane. Oil on canvas.
A Sandys, monogrammed.
12 x 18 ins., 30.5 x 45.7 cms.
This scene was painted by several artists
including D Hodgson, A Stannard and O Short.
A larger version by Sandys shows the river to the
right of the road and cottages. 'His' traveller
returning home features more than once,
reminding him of his days as a journeyman dyer
perhaps. The cottage on the left is what all the
artists found attractive, a similar study may be
spotted elsewhere in the book. Stannard's early
view in 1828 shows the cottage amongst trees, no
felled timber and the open road rather narrower –
before widening of the day!

Back of the Mill. Oil on oak panel. **A Sandys**
10 x 14 1/2 ins., 25.4 x 36.8 cms.
This title is written in pencil on the panel. It is a
midday scene on one of the Norwich rivers, with
the city showing in the distance. Sandys liked to
portray his figures carrying goods over a shoulder.
Swans, ducks and a rowing boat represent the
local, but not very active, river traffic.

next to each cottage, the detail of which is the same with bowing planks forming weatherboarded ends. Dare it be said that it is now apparent that only Anthony Sandys could have painted this kind of cladding, with the same bent boards? Sometimes, compressing paintings into hand-sized photographs is useful: if these two oil paintings were represented by just a couple of black and white photographs the similarities of outline would become quickly apparent. One would immediately be a clue to the other's identity, as indeed happened with the larger version already inscribed on the stretcher by A Sandys himself, and the smaller version purporting to be by H Bright through an incorrect attribution.

Norwich School artists had a habit of repeating themselves and, when they found a winning formula, they stuck to it. There is yet another recorded version of the 'windmill and cottage by a lane' scene. Sandys also had a way of slanting coloured strips of cloud across his sky at sunset, which the view of Norwich clearly displays.

By the very nature of his distinguishing colours, often used, Sandys had little need to sign many of his paintings. When he painted the wherry scene on the Norwich River and carefully monogrammed it 'AS' he fooled one owner into believing it was by Alfred Stannard, but the two styles of the painters are rather different. Perhaps more understandable is the confusion between Sandys and Alfred George Stannard, which occurs when the AS initials are sometimes spotted. Again, studying the paintings of each reveals the differences, but, even so, when Sandys painted a much duller view,

Overleaf page 66
Horses on the Marshes. Oil on canvas. **A Sandys**
9 1/2 x 14 5/8 ins., 24 x 37 cms.
The subject, with a wherry and highlights on the
fencing and elsewhere, shows several of the school
traits. The Yare or Waveney valley, at sunny
midday, a barn by a backwater used for storing
hay, is one of a number of valley views by Sandys.
The clouds appear very bright due to the subtle
use of a palette knife to smooth the paint, a
technique much used by H Bright whom he is
known to have copied.

with a pale blue and grey midday sky and no bright colours whatsoever, his name as the artist may not spring readily to mind.

The painting of skies often gives the artist away and, with Anthony Sandys and his evening skies, this is very much so. Two of the views, one of Whitlingham Lane and the other on the Broads, clearly show the mauve and crimson clouds straddled by a ribbon of white light, a feature of later paintings. With one of these paintings signed he had no need to initial the other. His 'Drainage Mill near Yarmouth' bears the same bright crimson too, this time of brickwork set alight by a late afternoon sun, which had also turned the marsh yellow, or so thought Anthony Sandys.

Anthony Sandy's works are considerably fewer than JB Ladbrooke's and so a pattern of signing is less easy to identify. The only two monograms referred to are in red. It happens that there is a larger version of the view at Whitlingham with the AS entwined on the butt end of a roadside log. Sandys had so contrived this dark monogram that it resembled a natural splitting of the wood, successfully disguising the fact that it was there at all. Even when a proper enquiry was made about the picture, already thought to be a Norwich School one, the artist was not identified! When Sandys lengthened his surname, inserting a 'y' around 1855, he may have decided he could play with his first name too. The small watercolour, which appears to be a study for the larger oil of a mill near Yarmouth, painted in the 1860s, is signed, surprisingly, Arthur Sandys (there is no record of an 'Arthur' anywhere else). The earliest dated landscape of his, the sunset view of Norwich, had a full inscription on the old stretcher with his name spelt Sands, and, in a corner of the picture, a faintly discernible pair of initials produced by indenting the wet paint with the wooden point of his brush – the remaining paintings illustrated are unsigned. Other oils have appeared sometimes with a monogram but rarely with a date. Bright and cheerful colour combinations, with a more thickly painted highlight on a windmill sail or rooftop, will probably remain Sandys' best signature.

Studying detail in a fine or broad sense will reap dividends, as so many Norwich paintings are unsigned. Once *au fait* with the general style of an artist, or family of artists, the perusal of this detail may then provide the clues that will reveal the artist's hand. With the Ladbrooke brothers this has certainly proved to be the case.

'Dunolly Sept 8'. Pencil Drawing. **A Sandys**
4 3/4 x 7 ins., 11.1 x 17.7 cms.
After visiting the Peak District in 1862 Sandys
went on to the west coast of Scotland, to Dunollie
Castle nr Oban, before climbing Ben Nevis and
returning home.

Marsh Mill nr Yarmouth. Oil on Winsor & Newton sketchboard. **A Sandys**
11 x 15 ins., 28 x 38.1 cms.
This colourful marsh landscape was painted after St Nicholas' Church, Gt Yarmouth, underwent restoration about 1862 with the addition of stone pinnacles to the tower. Said to be the largest parish church in England, its profile stands above the houses before it. The picture (it is related to Sandys' watercolour sketch of the mill) shows his love of colour with the late afternoon sunlight reflected in crimson and yellow. The water in the dyke is the same smooth blue as seen in the 'Norwich River' painting – Sandys and others liked to use colourful pigments wherever they could.

Drainage Mill nr Yarmouth. Watercolour on paper board. **A Sandys**, signed Arthur Sandys
5 3/4 x 7 3/4 ins. 14.6 x 19.6 cms.
There is no reason to suppose that this is by any other than Anthony, who anyway altered his surname in 1855. The oil painting version of the mill was completed in the 1860s, this watercolour being a preparatory study with the same pair of sails on the river to the left. 'Arthur' appears nowhere else, perhaps using it once was enough!

Five
Contemporary
society, school and
family painting

The Williams family · Suffolk and Norfolk Schools

THE DESIRE to study art, a growing engagement in the early part of the nineteenth century, brought about the formation of other societies and groups. The effect of the founding of London's Royal Academy in 1768 and the influx of paintings from the Continent, following the French Revolution, may have combined to spark this fresh interest in painting. Although no other provincial city has gained the longstanding reputation of giving rise to a school in quite the way that Norwich began to do so, in the first half of the nineteenth century, with the term 'Norwich School' so easily used in picture parlance today, it is important to look at other developments, however briefly.

Thomas Gainsborough moved from Suffolk to Bath in 1759, aged a little over thirty, and then painted there for some fifteen years. Alexander Cozens, who had studied in Italy, taught there in the 1760s. Later in the century Thomas Barker came to settle in Bath and through his painting he became permanently associated with the city, styling himself 'of Bath'. In 1808, a society, similar to Norwich's, was founded.

Bristol, too, had a number of well known artists such as Nicholas Pocock, William James Muller, and the famous Francis Danby who painted one of his best known paintings, 'The Avon Gorge', in 1822. Incidentally, the Rev James Bulwer from Norfolk did some of his painting in Bristol when he was a curate there up to 1820. It was not until the mid-1820s that the term Bristol School arose.

These two groups, and other societies in the north of England such as the ones in Leeds and Liverpool, all became established after the Norwich Society. However, they did not survive like the Norwich School; which serves to elevate its status, if need be! The late nineteenth century Norfolk School, sometimes so referred to, was successfully born of the Norwich School and deserves a passing mention.

In Suffolk a school of painting was slowly seen to emerge with Gainsborough and later Constable heralding its advent years in advance. Professional and amateur artists formed the first society in Ipswich in 1832.

Around this time in London the large Williams family of painters was becoming established as an important group. Both this, and the Suffolk School, have become of some significance to the study of the Norwich School because of their similarities.

THE WILLIAMS FAMILY

It can be quickly seen, looking at a handful of landscapes, that certain members of the Williams family closely mimicked the Norwich School painters. This was especially so with wooded lane subjects and watery scenes. For the very reason that the Williams family landscapes are confused with the Norwich School some are included in this book for comparison.

Certain members of the family must clearly have known Norwich painters and seen their exhibits in London. Furthermore they must have learnt even more about the painters and their works when they exhibited alongside them in Norwich in the 1840s and 50s. Eight of the twelve members, between them, are known to have sent fifty exhibits to Norwich.

Edward Williams (1782–1855), or 'Old' Williams, was the father of six well known painters. This list includes his eldest son Edward Charles (1807–1881) and Sidney Richard Percy Williams (1821–1886), perhaps the best known of all. Some of them altered their names. Henry John Williams (1811–1865) became instead a Boddington,

FACING PAGE TOP
SUFFOLK SCHOOL
Snow at the Inn. Oil on canvas. **Thomas Smythe**
(1825–1906), signed with initials
6 1/4 x 11 3/4 ins., 15.9 x 29.9 cms.
Thomas Smythe was at his best with his winter paintings – ice cold with blue. Snow scenes were not so common amongst Norwich School painters; H Bright did more than most, others the occasional one. This canvas has been laid on a pine panel, rather than being stretched, and was evidently marketed as such in kit form with frame to fit.

FACING PAGE BOTTOM
SUFFOLK SCHOOL
Village Cottages. Watercolour. **Thomas Smythe**
(1825–1906), signed indistinctly
11 1/4 x 16 1/2 ins., 28.6 x 41.9 cms.
If Thomas Smythe was not painting horses he was often recording cottage scenes like this, but usually in oils. Many of his dwellings were in dire need of repair! The painting shows he was a specialist in rendering colour detail of the fabric, perhaps more prominently than many of the Norwich artists were accustomed to do.

and Sidney Richard Williams called himself Percy and not Williams in his earlier years. These sons of 'Old' Williams produced five offspring who likewise painted landscapes. This resulted in there being three generations of Williams, rather like the Norwich generations with which they ran roughly in parallel, who could contribute confusion to the cause of the Norwich School a century on.

A more apt title for this chapter might have been 'Not the Norwich School'. With this in mind some of the differences will be pin-pointed. But first it must be stressed their similarities are often stronger than their differences, although the topographical scenes they sought out were usually away from Norfolk, but this was not so all the time. When they were in East Anglia they sometimes chose the same subjects, such as scenes in the Yare Valley. Furthermore, Old Williams, like John Crome, was influenced by the older Dutch School paintings which they both had copied. This they had done in the course of learning to paint. EC Williams, the son, continued to carry the Dutch woodland tradition in his early work and, for this reason, it happens that some of his work is confused with that of his father, who had taught him in the first place anyway. However, EC Williams' later works are quite distinctive. Like many Norwich paintings much of both their works is unsigned.

Three paintings by different members of the family are illustrated and are now the subject of discussion. Hopefully it can be shown that each has enough personality of its own for the viewer to spot that each is not a Norwich School picture.

Edwin Henry Boddington, the son of HJ Boddington born in 1836, painted the wide river view with two fishermen in a boat. There are cattle in the river and on the water meadow beyond. This probably dates to the 1850s and may well represent a scene on the river Yare near Surlingham. Boddington is known to have painted several views in Norfolk, amongst them exhibiting a 'View on the Yare' in 1855.

The only Norwich artist who perhaps comes near to Boddington, when viewing this painting, is Thomas Lound. But he would have given more colour and variety to the subject. The very clean outline of the tree-mass is not a Norwich attribute. The application of paint to the side slopes of the valley does not mate with a Norwich style. As a whole the rendering of the subject lacks the interest of a Norwich School painting; it is a little too flat. If, for example, Sandys had approached this subject, bearing in mind he painted at Whitlingham on the Yare, next door as it were, he would have livened up the sky and perhaps put a sailing craft mid-stream – a wherry or sailing boat. Norwich School figures tended to be colourful and this pair is not. A bright cap or tunic could have been looked for. Many Norwich painters also liked their River Yare to look blue! As it happens Boddington's work was usually better and more colourful than this.

The next painting to be analysed has altogether much more to be considered. It is a busy painting, colourful and detailed. The subject consists of cattle and a drover by a watermill, with the mill cottage very much catching the eye. Norwich School painters, such as JB Ladbrooke and WH Crome, painted watermills in Wales; in fact the frame of the painting bears a WH Crome gold label. However, it can be shown that the detail pulls away from members of the Norwich School and, one by one, Norwich artists can be eliminated. The painting bears little resemblance to the Ladbrookes; maybe in composition it does, but not in detail. One would be forgiven for thinking it was perhaps connected with George Vincent with trees in the middle – the central mass. The cattle and drover are reminders of him. But evidence of John Crome's teaching of

the use of colour to George Vincent is not there. Alfred Stannard often painted cottage scenes, and rooftops with problems like this one seems to have, but mill cottages in Wales are not reported to be amongst them. Several Norwich painters liked the use of white paint, for mid-distance mist, but they preferred a dark horizon, and not one such as this with white running up to it. So it is the detail that shows this painting is not by a Norwich School painter but is instead by EC Williams, painted most probably in the 1840s, as comparison of other subjects by him suggests.

Just as the Norwich School painters repeated themselves, and copied one another and other artists, so perhaps did members of the Williams family. After this painting, just described, was identified, a similar subject was found, also in Norfolk and not ten miles from Norwich, much more loosely painted and, even more clearly, not a Norwich painting. It is probably true to add that by the mid-1840s EC Williams would have seen plenty of Norwich School paintings and, as this illustrated painting shows, he was by then sharing some of the Norwich techniques. A look at the foliage detail shows this.

As so many books and catalogues concerning the Norwich School show mountains painted by the Crome family, Henry Bright, JB Ladbrooke and others, there is very good reason for including a Williams family view of Snowdon. This delightful picture by Walter Williams (1835–1906) was painted in the autumn of 1864. Of greatest importance, to iron out a difference from the Norwich School, is the fine – to a point of perfection – grass-work in the foreground. No Norwich School painter ever demonstrated this kind of attention to grass detail – trees maybe! From time to time H Bright tried to have a go. It is also true to say that the sky, all blue in oil paint without a cloud, is a singular non-Norwich event. The Norwich School painters doted on their skies. Walter Williams, no doubt, thought that with the eye focused on the complicated foreground construction the sky had to be plain. This is again of interest because the skies that he painted in his stormy coast scenes are second to none in the *œuvre* of Victorian painting and are collected for this reason. Few could capture an atmosphere so brilliantly as he; had he wanted a cloud formation over Snowdon he could very easily have had one.

It will always be easy to confuse some of the Williams family, and indeed other painters too, with certain members of the Norwich School. But sometimes it may prove useful not only to look for what is in a painting but also for what is not there – clouds and colours may be.

THE SUFFOLK SCHOOL

The Suffolk School owes its origins first to Gainsborough and then to Constable. This is not unlike the Crome, first, and Cotman, second, hierarchy in the Norwich School. However, as Ipswich lies only fifty miles from Norwich it would have been very surprising if the Norwich painters had not in some way influenced those just to the south. The Suffolk School, for part of its life, ran in tandem with the Norwich School, though, by the time the Smythe brothers and John Moore were beginning to paint, the Norwich School had been long established. Thomas Smythe (1825–1906) fell under Gainsborough's spell whereas his brother Edward Robert (1810–1899) was more influenced by the Norwich School. ER went to live in Norwich in 1840 and became friendly with Frederick Ladbrooke. Both friends later moved to Bury St Edmunds where they lived for twenty years, until F Ladbrooke died in 1865 and ER returned to

ENGLISH SCHOOL
The Old Watermill. Oil on canvas.
Edward Charles Williams (1807–1881)
16 x 23 ins., 40.6 x 58.4 cms.
This painting has many similarities to one of
his dated oils of 1846. For years a
WH Crome label was attached to the frame
which serves to illustrate the confusion,
which can easily occur, amongst members of
the Williams family and the Norwich School.
Differences are discussed in the text.

ENGLISH SCHOOL
River landscape. Oil on canvas.
EH Boddington (b.1836)
12 x 18 ins., 30.5 x 45.7 cms.
This is possibly a view on the Yare, one was
exhibited in 1855 by Edwin Henry, who was
one of the Williams family. The cows may be
at the edge of Postwick marsh. Bright
colours, familiar to the Norwich School, are
lacking. It is shown for comparison and
mentioned in the Williams section.

Ipswich. The Smythes' love of painting horses, far more prominently than the Norwich painters did their cows, is one of the features that makes their paintings so attractive. Snow scenes in the Norwich School were a bit of a rarity, although H Bright enjoyed doing them as did JB Ladbrooke in later life. Thomas Smythe, however, specialized in winter scenes. Somehow his portrayal of horses dragging timber through the snow, or folk trudging homeward to the warmth of their distant cottage, shows him in his finest form.

Thomas Churchyard (1798–1865) was influenced by both Constable and Crome whose works he collected and copied. There seems little doubt that John Moore (1820–1902) learnt a thing or two from the moonlight views painted by Crome's two sons. It is not uncommon for Moore's moonlight scenes to be credited to WH Crome, though the skies are not so appealing. This tends to occur when the influence of Gainsborough, in Moore's darkened foliage, is overlooked. Two moonlight views by Moore are illustrated; the larger one, showing the windmill, had a WH Crome label attached to it by its owner before the error was realised. The smaller view with the sheepdog, in many ways similar to the basic format of the larger one, shows blobby foliage. This should not be mistaken for the work of the Norwich School. It is worth noting that Colkett, H Ladbrooke, Joseph Paul, Vincent, WPB Freeman and Alfred Stannard painted moonlights for certain, besides all the Crome family too!

Robert Burrows, who was born in 1810, certainly must have looked over his shoulder at Norwich School paintings to the north, as there appears to be a similarity to those rather than to the likes of Constable and Gainsborough. He might easily have observed the works of Alfred Stannard.

FG Cotman is perhaps the most interesting link with Norwich for he was the nephew of John Sell Cotman. He was born in Ipswich in 1850 and entered the RA in 1868. There he proceeded to win the Gold Medal in 1873. To start with he was mainly a portrait painter turning later to landscapes with great success. His sometimes loose style of painting is illustrated here and is reminiscent of John Crome's 'Postwick Grove' in the Castle Museum. He also had another style which brings to mind some of the Hague School painters. He painted in Amsterdam in 1879, so it would seem likely he studied their works on such a visit. In 1899 he became President of the Ipswich Fine Art Club. This club had been founded twenty-five years earlier and was destined to continue flourishing, unlike two earlier enterprises which had been short-lived.

THE NORFOLK SCHOOL

The Norfolk School appears to be the title that takes over from the Norwich School to describe its followers towards the end of the century. By the 1870s and 80s the Norwich School output was dwindling away and a new style of painting was emerging. Around the rivers

of Norfolk and across the Broads watercolour painters like CH Harrison and SJ Batchelder were showing their hands. They painted from nature, no doubt inspired and influenced by the Norwich School painters. Perhaps several members of the Stannard family and the likes of Sandys and Lound, all river scene painters, were their chief guides. What John Crome had preached to them the new artists continued to practise.

Another artist of some repute, Robert Bagge Scott, was born in Norwich in 1849, the same year as Batchelder. Like several Norwich painters before him he travelled to the Continent to paint. His choice of scenery was rural Holland, and in particular the region of Dordrecht, whose waterfront he liked. During his time over there he met his future wife and learnt the styles of the Maris brothers and Mesdag. He was one of the founders of the Norwich Art Circle in 1886.

The Norwich School had boasted brilliant etchers. In their wake followed Charles John Watson (1846–1927), who helped Bagge Scott to found the Art Circle. CJ Watson could easily have been thinking of Thomas Lound when he drew and etched a 'Mill on the Fens' with Ely cathedral in the background, at the turn of the century. Fifty years earlier Lound had painted almost exactly the same scene.

These artists brought a new style and freshness to their paintings which happily lives on into the present century – Edward Seago landscapes are a classic example of this.

SUFFOLK SCHOOL
Sheep and Dog in Moonlight. Oil on oak panel. **John Moore** (1820–1902)
7 1/8 x 9 ins., 18 x 22.7 cms.
This is an example of the moonlight painter of the Suffolk School who used rather subdued colours, unlike the brighter ones of some of the Norwich School painters. The blobby foliage is also different.

River in Moonlight. Oil on oak panel.
Joseph Paul
6 x 10 7/8 ins., 15 x 27.5 cms.
*Paul was the copyist who 'stole'
many Crome and Stark views.
Several moonlights have confused
people into thinking of more
important artists than Paul – when
his style is hidden by darkness!*

SUFFOLK SCHOOL
Figures Walking by Moonlight. Oil on
mahogany panel. **John Moore**
(1820–1902)
9 1/8 x 11 3/4 ins., 23.2 x 29.8 cms.
*The composition of this painting is
not dissimilar to the smaller
moonlight by Moore. The slate-grey
cloud colour is typical. This
painting, for a long time, was
thought to be by WH Crome, whose
moonlights are mainly of river
scenes however.*

NORFOLK SCHOOL
Mill at Ely. Etching. **Charles John Watson** (1846–1927), signed on mount, dated 1901
7 x 10 ins., 17.8 x 25.4 cms.
The subject is reminiscent of Lound's Fenland paintings done fifty years earlier. Watson carried on the tradition of Norwich School etching in which many of the artists, it may not be known, had indulged.

NORFOLK SCHOOL
On the Bure, Runham. Watercolour on paper board. **CH Harrison** (1842–1902), signed, and inscribed on reverse
5 x 11 3/8 ins., 12.5 x 28.8 cms. (sight)
Looking up the river at sunset with a sailing boat, wherries and drainage mills. Artists like Lound and Sandys could easily have inspired Charles Harmony Harrison who, with Batchelder, went on a special trip along the Bure to sketch the river and its tributaries in 1880. The pair took over where the Norwich School ceased.

Six
The Continental
connection

The Barbizon School · The Hague School

AS ENGLISH landscape painting gathered momentum, advancing into the nineteenth century, it is interesting and worthwhile to look at how painting developed on the nearby Continent. Just as the Norwich School had evolved in England so, too, did two important national schools of painting across the Channel, the first named after a village and the second after a city. The Barbizon School sprang up not far from Paris towards the middle of the century, in the village that gave its name to the group; later on, the Hague School followed it in Holland. Just as the flow of Norwich School paintings at home began to ebb, around 1870, so the Hague output swelled. The evolution of Barbizon painting is not dissimilar to that of Norwich. It is even a fact that certain English painters, and probably one in particular, may have influenced its development. Their chief similarities were based on their great leanings towards the old Dutch masters of landscape and the newfound belief in painting from nature. Perhaps one or two members of the Norwich School made a small but recognisable contribution to the refreshing mentality of both of these new schools.

Norwich School painters had always associated themselves with both France and Holland. In 1814 John Crome visited Paris to see the looted pictures in the Louvre following the fall of Napoleon – Crome's famous view in Paris, 'Italian Boulevard', was a result of this visit. After the Battle of Waterloo there was the chance to travel freely between England and France. John Crome's son, John Berney, with George Vincent, travelled there in 1816. John Sell Cotman went on touring trips in Normandy between 1817 and 1820. Others, like John Berney Ladbrooke, went there too. It should also be mentioned that famous artists such as Girtin and Turner had visited France early in the century; Bonington settled there after Napoleon's fall.

The start of the nineteenth century saw painting from nature becoming a theme. John Constable, like John Crome, was expanding the idea. It was at the Paris Salon exhibition of 1824, when several English landscape painters had works on display, that John Constable stole the show. His work was so well received that he was rewarded with a gold medal by the King, Charles X, after which his work was hung in a place of honour. The two large paintings which had proved so successful were 'View on the Stour' and 'The Haywain'. The impetus of this fresh style of painting gave further inspiration, it seems, to certain students of French romantic painting.

The Barbizon School, yet to be named, was slowly seen to develop some years after this event in a village on the outskirts of the extensive hunting grounds of Fontainebleau. If any one figure gained credit for the evolution of this school, like John Crome of the Norwich School, it has to be Pierre Henri de Valenciennes, a landscape artist who produced a lengthy book on landscape painting, first published in 1800 to be followed by a second edition in 1820, a year after his death. He extolled the virtues of painting from nature and even recommended to his pupils that they should look to the big forests to paint, mentioning Fontainebleau amongst them! So the school sprung up practising its painting in and around the large forest of Fontainebleau in the 1830s and 40s, the artists being able to live or stay in the village made famous by them. Though the school did have a style of its own, this was one with which many Norwich School followers would have been familiar – wooded landscapes with cattle, windmills in river landscapes, or figures on a country lane. The paintings were of fine quality; soon figureheads like Corot and Millet emerged. One artist who painted many woodland scenes, so typical of the Norwich School, was Theodore Rousseau. The art critic T Gautier had this to say of one of Rousseau's paintings of 1840, 'L'Allée des

DUTCH SCHOOL
A View nr Delft. Oil on panel. **Johan Barthold Jongkind** (1819–1891), signed and dated 1844
9 ¹/4 x 12 ³/8 ins., 23.5 x 31.5 cms.
This painting is shown for the interesting basic similarity it has with A Sandys' painting 'The Norwich River'. A pupil of Andreas Schelfhout, at the Hague Drawing Academy, Jongkind did many river and canal scenes. Born in Holland he moved to Paris in 1846; he later became a famous forerunner of Impressionism. (Reproduced from the Haags Gemeentemuseum Collection, The Hague, with photograph kindly supplied)

BARBIZON SCHOOL
Sheep on the edge of Woodland. Oil on canvas.
Charles Emile Jacques (1813–1894)
21 ¹/4 x 25 ³/4 ins., 54 x 65.4 cms.
Jacques did several variations of this subject which may be meant to represent sheep by the forest of Fontainebleau. He was a renowned expert at painting sheep, in their natural surroundings, making more of them than the Norwich School ever attempted. He also achieved success with rich colouring and highlights; it is interesting to compare his pastoral scenes with those in Norfolk, done about the same time. Jacques is known, too, for his brilliant etchings.

Chataigniers': 'In this incomparable work Theodore Rousseau recalls the robust Hobbema – whilst remaining indisputably original – and the powerful master generally referred to by the English as 'Old Crome'. Never has nature been observed from close by and rendered expansively with such an intense effect and such profound and genuine poetry.' (*The Barbizon School*, 1985, John Sillevis, Hans Kraan).

In Holland, again following the fall of Napoleon, there had developed a renewed interest in art which in recent times had been at a low ebb. King William I became patron of the Hague Academy in 1814, which resulted in the first public exhibition of a wide range of art occurring in the Hague. Two of the students at the time were Andreas Schelfhout (1787–1880) and Bart van Hove (1790–1880). These two, through their pupils, were to play an important part in the subsequent formation of the Hague School. Schelfhout was an accomplished landscape painter who painted many winter scenes, van Hove was on the teaching staff of the Academy and concentrated on town scenes. Later B van Hove was elected chairman of the newly founded Pulchri Studio ('for the study of beauty') in the Hague in 1847 – this was to become a well known artists' club involving many Hague School painters.

By the 1850s and 60s it was quite apparent in Holland that the Barbizon School was being closely observed by the painters in the Hague. It was yet to be named the Hague School; this did not occur until 1875 when an art critic gave it the title. Like the Norwich School it came to involve several generations of painters. Judging from the style of painting it would seem that the Hague School, which grew to maturity during the last two decades of the nineteenth century, did so really on its own merits. It is, however, well known that the members of the Barbizon and Hague Schools met and exchanged ideas. One of the first to fall under the influence of the Barbizon School was Willem Roelofs. Later, as if to emphasise the joint interest, HW Mesdag, one of the leading members of the Hague School, formed a large number of Hague and

The Pollarded Tree. Oil on canvas. **WH Crome**
8 1/4 x 10 1/4 ins., 20.9 x 26 cms.
A Norfolk landscape belonging to his green period. The small splashes of white and brown mid-distance show cows in a manner featured in some of his paintings. Likewise the quarter view of a pond in the foreground is another characteristic. His better artistic abilities should not be overlooked.

DUTCH SCHOOL
Girl in a Woodland Clearing. Oil on mahogany panel.
Anthonie Jacobus van Wijngaerdt (1808–1887),
signed
5 ⁷/₈ x 7 ⁷/₈ ins., 15 x 20.1 cms.
*This illusration is included to give an example of
a woodland painting on the Continent in the
middle of the last century. Wijngaerdt was an
accomplished artist whose open landscapes, with
farm buildings or animals, and woodland scenes
were typical of the period and similar to Norwich
subjects. Many different shades of green make up
the mix of the wood, much in the same way as
occurs in WH Crome's paintings.*

FACING PAGE
HAGUE SCHOOL
Cows in Polder Country. Black chalk and watercolour.
Anton Mauve (1838–1888), signed
11 ³/4 x 8 ⁵/8 ins., 29.8 x 21.9 cms.
This picture typifies the Hague 'grey' period, as it is referred to. In his case Anton Mauve would rather it had been spoken of as the 'silver' period; it is easy to see why. A sombre yet supreme example.

Norwich River Scene. Oil on mahogany panel.
R Ladbrooke (attr.)
7 ¹/4 x 6 ³/4 ins., 18.4 x 17.2 cms.
This dark Dutch influenced landscape is probably the earliest in the book. Further research may reveal the pale spotted foliage, and grey-white sky, river and buildings are indeed signs of Old Ladbrooke's early to mid-period work. Compare the 'tree' arrangement with HL's 'Road to the Valley'.

Barbizon School paintings into a collection. Today the museum that houses this array of paintings is worthy of a visit – Museum Mesdag in the Hague.

So, as the second half of the nineteenth century moved on, many views by very mature and brilliant artists of the Dutch landscape were increasingly appearing. Cattle in meadows under pollarded willows, or sheep in a lane with a shepherd, as well as shore scenes and seascapes were commonplace. To begin with this was roughly in parallel with subjects produced by second generation and younger artists of the more parochial Norwich School, each having its own rather similar appeal. As time went on the Hague School developed its grey, or silver, period where polder country was depicted in sombreness. This became its hallmark.

So it can be seen how the fundamental Dutch influence of early landscape painting brought about the development of three successive schools, not to mention the German School. The new interpretation of landscape painting by English artists had percolated its way into French romantic art, focusing around Fontainebleau, where it had expanded. Artists in Holland observed the new theme of things and, with a fresh rendering of ideas, followed suit. That there were links between the schools, however slender and spiritual these may have been, seems to be evident, though the stature of the Norwich School was perhaps only sufficient to bring forth the influence of the two chiefs – Crome and Cotman. Later however, artists travelled more frequently between England, Holland, and France, making it interesting to observe, for example, the similarities of some watercolours by FG Cotman, John Sell Cotman's nephew, to those of a prominent member of the Hague School, Anton Mauve. It is too simple an explanation to say that artistic thinking had gone a full circle, from the time Crome and Constable had set to work to that of the returning influence from Holland, but even so the Continental connection can be seen to be there – encompassed in a century of time.

A Pastiche. Oil on board. **H Ladbrooke**,
monogrammed HL, dated 1847
20 x 24 ins., 50.8 x 61 cms.
Henry here has copied a Flemish painting;
another likeness by a different 19th century
painter exists. His brother JBL also copied
Continental subjects, sometimes turning them into
'Norwich'-looking pieces! The zig-zag branch
work and the corner detail are both evident. HL
was unable, sometimes, to paint cows as well as
his brothers could.

Seven
Confusion in class

Who painted what? A close look

A Country Lane. Oil on mahogany panel. **JB Crome**
11¹/4 x 8¹/4 ins., 28.5 x 21 cms.
This picture well shows how Norwich School muddles have developed, and from within the School too! A letter of 1871 written by J B Ladbrooke and glued to the back states the painting is by his uncle Old Crome when, in fact, it is by his cousin. The nature of the tree trunk, split at the base, and the snaking wheelrut, filled with stones, can be seen in other JBC oils - 'Rouen' and 'Burgh Castle' respectively (NCM). Reproduced by courtesy of Felder Fine Art, photo by Prudence Cumming Associates Ltd., both of London.

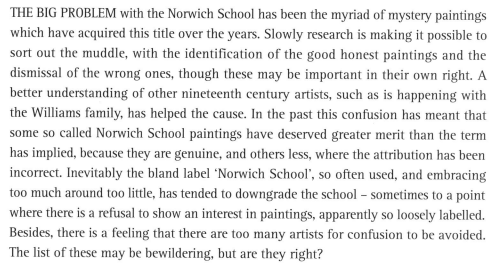

Facing page
View at Colney. Oil on millboard. **H Ladbrooke**
14 x 12 ins., 35.5 x 30.5 cms.
This is H Ladbrooke's interpretation of the view which many artists painted following J Crome's example. The low branch of the oak tree in the foreground is utterly characteristic of Henry – zig-zagged into segments (tipped sideways it looks like a hedgehog). The colouring of a pair of trees in two differing tones is a common feature in the School. Plant life, in a bottom corner, is another sign of Henry's work and so is the smoke flowing from the chimneys. A few green sheep are just visible; the colouring of his figure should be noted. The sandy nature of the soil in Norfolk made for attractively coloured banks.

Bothy. Oil on canvas. **JB Ladbrooke**
10 x 8 ins., 25.4 x 20.3 cms.
'An unfinished picture' is inscribed on the back of this Ackermann & Co. stretcher. JB painted several stone-built watermills around 1850 (e.g. Overshot Mill, Ambleside). This bothy of slate and stone, partly covered by a climbing rose, may be a memory of a visit to the Lake District or Wales. The figure, painted almost like a jig-saw fit of several pieces, with drooping shoulders, is not untypical of his style; nor is the linear leaf work on the left.

THE BIG PROBLEM with the Norwich School has been the myriad of mystery paintings which have acquired this title over the years. Slowly research is making it possible to sort out the muddle, with the identification of the good honest paintings and the dismissal of the wrong ones, though these may be important in their own right. A better understanding of other nineteenth century artists, such as is happening with the Williams family, has helped the cause. In the past this confusion has meant that some so called Norwich School paintings have deserved greater merit than the term has implied, because they are genuine, and others less, where the attribution has been incorrect. Inevitably the bland label 'Norwich School', so often used, and embracing too much around too little, has tended to downgrade the school – sometimes to a point where there is a refusal to show an interest in paintings, apparently so loosely labelled. Besides, there is a feeling that there are too many artists for confusion to be avoided. The list of these may be bewildering, but are they right?

Looking more closely at individual artists, one problem that emerges is the similarity of the scenes each chose to paint; many artists often made use of identical subjects. When this happened there was of course a different emphasis placed here and there, for no two artists painted the same way, even when making a faithful copy. A small but typical example of this is the 'View at Colney', which was originally painted by John Crome and later by both Henry and JB Ladbrooke. A fourth version has now appeared by David Hodgson; there could well be others. However, for years real confusion existed over two of the three subsequent Colney views, the work by H Ladbrooke being attributed to George Vincent and that by Hodgson to John Crome himself! As a museum curator once so nicely put it: "We have two Cromes in our collection but we are not sure who they are by." So the question often arises as to how best can the problem of authorship be overcome.

It must be quite obvious that being familiar with paintings, as many as possible, is the only real method. New knowledge can be gained by searching out museum collections and their reserve ones, auctions where Norwich paintings are known to appear, and books, catalogues and collections of photographs. It *is* useful to study photographs and plenty of them. These compress the picture into an easily absorbable quantity. And, if gathered in numbers on particular artists, afford a ready and useful supply of information, which will help when comparing the subjects and styles of one artist with another. Often such photographs are in black and white and, although the important colours are missing, the subject content from tree shapes to figure and animal profiles can be studied.

Some collections of photographs have been built up over many years, and it would not be wrong to suggest that there may be several misfits

in large ones. If one hundred 'James Starks' were to be handled. one or two would probably prove to be by each of the following: Colkett, JB Ladbrooke, Vincent, Alfred Stannard and a couple of members of the Williams family. The reasons for this are fairly obvious but become more so when it is realised that Colkett, for example, was not only a pupil of J Stark but copied some of his paintings. 'Old' Williams likewise produced some very Stark-like compositions – both he and Stark having copied Hobbema's style – as did Williams' son Edward Charles. Others, like Alfred Stannard, produced similar wooded subjects.

It is instructive to look for individual characteristics. James Stark once owned a dog called 'Trim' and, judging from the small oil he did of his dog curled up asleep, this was a King Charles spaniel. Some wooded landscape views by Stark show a similar spaniel placed beside a group of gypsies or countryfolk. He probably owned the dog in midlife as these paintings are of the earlier Windsor period; he moved to Windsor in 1839. In his former Norwich period, when he was painting a flock, he sometimes showed a dog like a collie, similar to the dog that Alfred Stannard used to portray. With all the sheep in East Anglia this was hardly surprising. Some Norwich School artists depended on animals and it is not difficult to see how George Vincent painted his cows, or how Colkett painted his, or his sheep for that matter. Obadiah Short used to gather his sheep together in a tight flock as if they were heading straight for his easel.

With so many animals around it was to be expected that the artists would paint the fences and gates which were meant to keep these cherished animals in their proper places. Where these are found even they will have their traits. JB Ladbrooke's gates were always simpler than Alfred Stannard's, whose complicated construction often ran to five or six bars. Another detail is frequently seen in the foreground where many of the artists used to place a log or two; each one of them painted logs a different way using their own shapes and colours. It may seem a bizarre way of spotting an artist by his wayside timber, but it can be done!

Some years ago a painting appeared in London confidently attributed to James Stark and sold as such. In the foreground of this beautiful composition lay an old, slightly bowed, decaying log that only George Vincent could have placed there. One Norwich School painter who was not much inclined to put simple logs in his paintings was in fact James Stark. He did on occasions of course, colourfully painted much like his tree trunks. He was more intent, however, on making a feature of felled timber – whole trunks with branches and men working around them. This was so in his Windsor period, no doubt inspired by sights in the forest, just as his son was too.

Naturally it is important to learn something of signatures, especially which ones are more likely to be genuine. There was once a habit, it seems, of adding signatures to Norwich School paintings, because so often the artists left the original unsigned. Sometimes the painting acquired the correct name in this way, and sometimes not, but either way it gained a false signature. Occasionally one artist copied another. One example seen of this was a small view of St Benedict's Abbey which bore H Bright's name but was plainly painted by A Sandys, adopting a Bright subject and signing so. However these are more exceptions than rules. Most signatures on works of lesser artists are likely to be genuine as there was no great incentive to forge either the signatures or their works. More often than not it is now the lack of signatures that causes so many problems. Few artists, of what was then a new school, apparently saw a need to sign – little knowing the help it would have been in later years – or keep records.

FACING PAGE BOTTOM
Pair of Landscapes. Oil on panel. **A Stannard**
6 x 5 ins., 15.2 x 12.7 cms.
Compositions with cottages and water, one showing Norwich cathedral far off. Contemporary copies of this pair were made by another artist, probably SV Hunt of Norfolk judging from their looks, which escaped into the art world labelled as genuine Stannards – before this pair reappeared.

Cottage by a Wooded Lane.
Oil on oak panel.
A Stannard
*11 1/4 x 15 ins., 28.6 x 38.1
cms.*
*This is an early oil, which
needed restoration,
showing his compact style
compared with the later
loose one. The scene is
based on J Stark's
upright oil painting
study, and his etching of
1822, and is likely to
have been completed not
long afterwards during
the 1820s. Alfred did a
number of covered lane
scenes, such as
Whitlingham Lane with
the tree-tops kissing,
putting his own mark
upon them – the five-bar
gate, the dog and the girl
with the 'sun-hat'!*

Some Norwich School artists, however, enjoyed hiding their monograms or signatures, feeling perhaps lettering would spoil the effect of the picture. George Vincent often did this, placing a GV on the stern of a boat or the side of a pitcher. On one memorable occasion an argument developed over a painting that had some curious characteristics – a river scene on the Yare with bright and unusual foliage. Thomas Lound had been spoken of; but George Vincent had faithfully recorded himself by placing a G and a V, very discreetly, on the flaps of the canopy of the fishing boat, the centrepiece of the picture. This fact stared everyone in the face before it was eventually spotted; the disguise in the folds had worked!

David Hodgson, who painted many town views of Norwich, Chester and York, often showed shops in his street scenes. Rather than sign openly on the roadside, or worse, in the gutter, he would sometimes tuck his name above a shop doorway, as if he was the proprietor, or place his initials on the side of the delivery cart parked alongside. Alfred Stannard at times used a log, or, in his sea pieces, a floating piece of driftwood on which to place his name always very carefully in case it sank perhaps! Important Norwich pictures have, more than a few times, been found to have their signatures hidden with warm discussion resulting over authorship. A spot of bright light may be needed to reveal a dark signature on a muddy road, or riverbank, or one lost in the shadows of a moonlit night.

Several hundred artists exhibited at Norwich, but it is really only the better names with which the term Norwich School can usefully be applied, if it is to have meaning like the terms Barbizon and Hague School imply in their own countries. Dividing up these better artists into their main categories of painting – portrait, landscape, seascape and still life – may help when searching for a name, if the overlap is not too much of a problem. The style of a painting may then give a clue as to whether it is likely to be early, mid or late Norwich School. Its frame may be helpful. By a process of elimination there need be only a handful of names to consider. Without a painting's full history there may always be confusion, and it must not be forgotten that Norwich School painters, like all others, experimented.

A collection of John Middleton's work, handed down through a branch of the family, contained two watercolours of a few shrubs in loosely painted little landscapes, probably done as quick studies. They were quite out of keeping with the rest of the collection – these two on their own would have caused a muddle for ever without their provenance. If one artist named Rembrandt continues to prove difficult for scholars then it is no wonder that much research is needed into a classful of Norwich School names. As in a climate of chaos, once cloud patterns are established forecasting becomes possible. It's a challenge!

Farmstead, Returning Home. Oil on canvas.
A Stannard
12 x 15 1/4 ins., 30.5 x 38.7 cms.
This composition is interesting for being unusual.
It is a late period painting where low sunlight has
been used to create brightness on clouds and trees
otherwise in the shadows. Stannard often brushed
a ribbon along cloud edges to achieve this, like
Sandys did. Note the unicorn on the horse, one of
Alfred's quaint touches, the crude but complicated
gate and the blue horizon with its windmill.

Sheep Dipping at Trowse Mill Norwich *(detail – full picture overleaf)*. Oil on canvas.
A Stannard, signed Alfred Stannard P and dated 1839 (P:Pinxit, title on frame)
44 x 69 ins., 111.7 x 175.2 cms.
This important painting, although illustrated in other books, is reproduced in
colour as it contains much magnificent detail. It is worth noting the spaghetti-like
spread of willow foliage, the unicorn adorning the mill roof, the six bar gate and
the dotted highlights. The same sluice gate appears in his earlier painting 'Sluice
Gate on the Wensum'- with a church tower in place of the mill. Artistic licence!
(Reproduced by kind permission of Nestle UK Ltd.)

93

Eight
Frames and labels

Dating and placing a painting: looking for clues

Label by R Ladbrooke, jnr; 1830s

Label by R Ladbrook (sic); 1820s

Label by Rowney & Foster; 1820s

Label by Townshend; 1850s

NO PAINTING looks complete unless embellished by a frame. All too often frames are taken for granted. Many people visiting an art gallery may remember the paintings but are unlikely to recollect much of the frames. This is not to say that frames are taken completely for granted, for the same people would be aghast suddenly to find paintings hanging unframed. Many frames were extravagantly designed in an ornate fashion to complement the picture. One of the pleasures of touring the Castle Museum in Norwich is to see the paintings adorned in beautiful, and mostly original, frames – made to measure years ago. It must be remembered that frames were chosen by the collectors of the day, so that what is admired now was a popular choice in their time too. Indeed, the substantial sums of money that are needed to buy high quality period gilt frames today show that tastes have not changed.

The hidden history that may be glued to the back of an old picture is worth hunting for. The unsigned painting on the book cover, still hanging in what must be its original frame from around 1825, should be turned around. A tiny label, quaintly shaped, on the back reveals the name of the framemaker and thereby hints at the artist. This label is a rarity and reads:

> R Ladbrook
> Carver Gilder Picture and Looking Glass
> Framemaker, White Lion Street, Norwich.

Lady, as later portrayed in the landscape of 1836. Pencil drawing and watercolour. **HB Love**, signed and dated 1835

10 x 7 7/8 ins., 25.4 x 20 cms.
One picture without the other would not tell a story; fortunately the two never became separated! The lady first appeared in a lovely rosewood frame and later, for her landscape setting, in a gilt one. She certainly meant something to someone! The only clue to her identity is the name 'Sewell' written on the back of her landscape, and on component parts of the contemporary Freeman gilt frame, presumably as it was made up.

What better than for JB Ladbrooke, who neither ended his name with an 'e' in early life, to have pinched one of his brother's frames in which to display the painting! Presumably Robert Ladbrook's framing business flourished as otherwise his son, also known as Robert (to avoid confusion: old Robert Ladbrook's grandson), would not have followed in his footsteps. The first record that this self-styled Robert Ladbrooke 'junior' was a Norwich framemaker comes from a label on a wooden frame containing an HB Love portrait, dated 1837. That he was a craftsman is revealed by the quality of the frame constructed of rosewood veneer. Besides framemaking, the younger Ladbrooke was also a picture restorer; he later moved to Yarmouth.

Another Love portrait has been found in a maple wood finished frame. This fashionable piece of veneering was done by the Cabinet and Picture Frame Manufactory (sic) belonging to GR Miller on St Andrew's Hill, Norwich, as a label on the back of the almost miniature frame testifies.

Probably the most famous Norwich framer of all, and one of the most pleasing watercolourists, was John Thirtle. He produced many fine quality decorative frames with enough labels still attached today to show the extent of his business. Early labels were of a simple design; later ones have been found with distinctively different bordered

Lady in a landscape. Watercolour and bodycolour. **HB Love**, initialled HBL, dated 1836
8 ³/₈ x 6 ⁵/₈ ins., 21.2 x 16.8 cms.
The thin smooth card-like paper is watermarked Ruse & Turner 1823(?). A sheen shows where gum
arabic has been used to highlight the darker colours of hair and dress (folds). Love was one of the
most successful portrait painters of the School, preferring a miniature style. The unknown sitter
was drawn a year earlier by him as well, perhaps before her betrothal as she sported no rings on
that occasion. Love painted a few landscapes; this painting affords a rare glimpse of his abilities.

edges. One of these later ones, attractively designed with a blue tint to it, describes his business accordingly:

> *John Thirtle*
>
> *Picture Frame & Looking Glass*
>
> *Manufacturer*
>
> *Wholesale and Retail*
>
> *Magdalen Street*
>
> *Norwich*

This label is on a frame around a Henry Ladbrooke landscape. The painting itself is on a millboard which bears the caption:

> *Improved*
>
> *Flemish Ground Mill'd Boards*
>
> *prepared by*
>
> *G Rowney & Co*
>
> *artists' colourmen*
>
> *51 Rathbone Place*

The firm George Rowney and Company adopted this label in 1837. Thirtle's business, as such, ceased in 1839 when he died and W Boswell took it over. It is fair to suggest these two labels, and nothing else, provide a likely date for the painting – at the end of the 1830s.

W Boswell no doubt wanted to demonstrate that he had acquired Thirtle's business, and so his early labels are distinguished by the addition of 'Late Thirtle' in brackets. Once established he dropped this reference and remarked instead that he had the largest collection of antique oil paintings in the Eastern Counties. This grander and more elaborate label recorded that W Boswell was a carver, gilder, upholsterer, cabinet and chair maker of 48 London St. It mentioned 'artists' colourmen' and 'the best house for first class furniture, looking glasses, paper hangings etc.' besides repairing old furniture.

Another framer, whose work is often enough encountered, was Samuel T Townshend who set himself up in Charing Cross, Norwich, in 1851. Some of his frames are most delicately moulded.

Dimmock & Son were also known to be working in London St, no. 66, around 1870 in their Fine Art Galleries.

However one of the framers who was most prominent when John Crome began to paint was Jeremiah Freeman. Later, about 1830, the firm's work was described in great detail:

> *Freeman, Carver Gilder & Looking Glass Manufacturer, Wholesale and*
> *Retail, London & Swan Lane, Norwich on Terms Low as any House in the*
> *United Kingdom, The Greatest Number & Variety of Looking Glasses (sic),*
> *Concave and Convex Mirrors, Lustre Lamps, Candelabri, Bronzes, Fire*
> *Screens and Stands, Picture and Print Frames Highly ornamented or plain*
> *Gold Borders for Rooms etc. Plate Glass of a Superior Colour & Substance*
> *for Drawing Room Windows, Carriages, Shop Fronts etc. Old Glasses*
> *ground, Polished, Silvered and Framed. Workmen sent to any part of the*
> *Kingdom. An extensive Collection of Prints by the most esteemed Masters*
> *of all Nations, Ancient & Modern. Pictures carefully Cleaned and*
> *Preserved, every requisite for Painting, Drawing and fancy Work. Full*
> *value given, for Pictures, Old Prints & other Works of Art.*

In 1922 W Boswell & Son produced a booklet headed *Art in Picture Restoring*. A descendant of the Boswell family has kindly supplied the Norwich Castle Museum with a copy from where the following is reproduced:

> *Established in 1725, nearly two hundred years ago, long before the days of the famous Norwich School of Painting, when Crome, Cotman, Stark, and Vincent held their meetings in the then well-known meeting places.*
>
> *This firm has been carried on by three well-known families, Thirtle, Freeman, and Boswell.*
>
> *Thirtle was a well-known frame maker, and the maker of the now famous swept frame, which has never been equalled, he also was, and still is an artist of no small repute. Many of his drawings are now in the safe keeping by the Norwich Castle museum and other National and Civil galleries. He also was a restorer of old pictures, and much of his work returns to present members of the firm after a great many years.*
>
> *The business was carried on in Magdalen Street up to his death in 1839, when the business was taken over by Mr William Boswell.*
>
> *Freeman carried on his business at 2, London Lane, now London Street. There were many generations of this old Norwich family, many of them taking a very active part in the public life in the City of Norwich, William becoming Mayor of the City in 1843.*
>
> *Here again the art of frame making and picture restoring was carried on with the greatest of success. And today business tickets are very often seen on the back of old famous pictures.*
>
> *This business was taken over in 1870 by W Boswell, who was born in 1810, serving his apprenticeship with William Freeman, and in turn took up the reins of the two businesses in 1839 and 1870, when he took over Freeman's business in London Street.*
>
> *He not only was a great frame maker and restorer of old pictures, but was the great expert on all artists of the Norwich School, having many of the now famous and valuable pictures by Crome, Cotman etc., through his hands. William Boswell died in 1877.*

The pamphlet next describes how the business was carried on by his two sons Samuel and James.

It is important to realise that it was not only the firms of Norwich which provided for the artist. W Spanton worked in Abbey Gate Street, Bury St Edmunds, framing Frederick Ladbrooke's paintings. He also did this for Frederick's friend ER Smythe, which helped to solve the problem on one occasion as to whether a dirty landscape was by him or his brother Tom who lived in Ipswich – the frame bore a W Spanton stamp. Moving in the other direction, EB Freeman left the Norwich business and set himself up in Deneside, Great Yarmouth.

Further away in London, Ackermann provided frames and materials to the Norwich artists; and Roberson and Co., of Long Acre, supplied millboards to Thomas Lound. As more evidence of the capital's connection, a late period JJ Cotman oil was found in a Colnaghi frame, a lovely swept one bearing a label with the address Pall Mall East, which made the owner think the painting was nothing to do with the Norwich School!

Portrait of a Horse. Oil on canvas. **CJW Winter**, signed and dated 1844
15 x 18 ins., 38.1 x 45.7 cms.
Winter, who was born in Bungay, lived close to Beccles where Edwin Cooper, the horse painter also lived. There is little doubt that Cooper greatly influenced his horse painting. About 1844 Winter moved to Yarmouth, accepting commissions, perhaps painting this as one of them. Faint pencilling between the front hooves may be the horse's name! Note the round tower of the Norfolk church behind the horse's domain.

Thorpe next Norwich. Watercolour. **John Joseph Cotman**, inscribed and dated on label 1868
5 1/8 x 7 3/4 ins., 13 x 19.6 cms. (sight)
This painting is of considerable interest as it reveals the location of JB Ladbrooke's 'Landscape – the Rustic Bridge' illustrated in Dickes' book and which is on permanent display in the Castle Museum. This JBL picture is also featured in Cundall's Studio, The Norwich School, 1920, when it goes by the name of 'The Sluice Gate'. For JJ Cotman's composition, however, the sluice gate has been demolished. JBL's painting of 1869 is based on his own pencil drawing which he signed and dated 1852 (itself exhibited in 1975 by Oscar and Peter Johnson).

Once again, returning to the cover picture, it is interesting to note the label on the reverse which reads 'Improved Flemish Ground Milled Boards, Rowney & Foster'. This title was used for the firm's name from 1817 until 1837. A number of Norwich School millboards bear Ackermann & Co. labels of 96 Strand, London, which dates these boards to 1830–1856. At the same time Ackermann used a stamped imprint on wooden stretchers bearing similar information.

Ackermann was an interesting business. At the start of the 19th century it was engaged in a variety of enterprises – painting, printing, publishing and designing. Later on, as far as the Norwich School was concerned, it published James Sillett's *Grammar of Flower Painting* about 1820 and *Ackermann's Rudimentary Drawing Book for Beginners* by H Bright in 1843. And the Regents Street branch of the firm 'The Eclipse Sporting Gallery', so-named in 1829, published two lithographs of Edwin Cooper's work.

Winsor & Newton millboards can be dated by their Royal Appointments. A board most commonly found has a label declaring 'Artists' Colourmen to Her Majesty and to His Royal Highness Prince Albert' – this was used between 1841 and 1857. Winsor and Newton itself was established in 1832 at 38, Rathbone Place. In 1878 a 'W' was added to the London address, which sometimes helps to date a very late Norwich School painting.

The study of paper used for drawing and painting is altogether another subject, but it is worth mentioning the materials and marks that are found.

Cartridge paper, so-called because of its use to contain a gun charge, was first advertised by Ackermann for mounting and sketching in 1802. Board paper, in texture like a modern visiting card, appeared early in the century too. This thick paper was better to paint on than the thin paper before it as it did not so easily buckle, or cockle, when wet. Ackermann produced a quality white variety for use instead of ivory board. Sometimes several pieces of paper were fixed together to form a (thicker) board. Some of this was so well made that it appears to be one sheet, the laminations invisible. A few of the pictures shown are on one kind of 'paper board' or another. Millboards, in common use and much cheaper than canvases, were originally made from many sheets of brown paper stuck together with gelatin and pressed in a mill – hence 'milled'. Watercolour and drawing paper was often 'labelled' with a clear watermark, which is why it is referred to as 'Whatman' paper in common parlance. Much of it was not white owing to the materials it was made from, which included old rope and sailors' shirts! Holding these old pieces of paper up to bright light may reveal, besides the maker's name, a very useful date.

Thus, small seemingly simple bits of information may show the way to the origin of a painting. Finally it is worth commenting that framing tastes have changed in respect of watercolours, for today fine swept gilt frames are always associated with oil paintings. However, an aquatint of the fourth annual exhibition of the Society of Painters in Watercolours, 1808, in Old Bond Street (Ackermann's: the microcosm of London 1808–10) shows all the watercolours displayed in large swept gilt frames!

Frame by Robert Ladbrooke; 1820s

Frame by Thirtle; 1830s

Frame by Townshend; 1850s

Frame by Boswell; 1870s

Nine
A special collection

JB Ladbrooke: an analysis

A DELIGHTFUL GROUP of half a dozen oil paintings displayed on the dining room wall of a house in Norfolk has provided us with a wonderful opportunity to study some middle period works of JB Ladbrooke. These delicate little studies clearly portray the very essence of the school by showing rustic views captured in the Norfolk countryside, or, if derived from his imagination, inspired by seeing similar such scenes. All that is known of this collection is that it was acquired, with the addition of one other painting, by an ancestor of the present owner around the middle of the last century. Whether the Norfolk family knew JB Ladbrooke, or not, is unknown and all that can be said with certainty about their date is that the board on which the heath landscape is painted dates from 1841 to 1857 – this being the period for the particular Winsor and Newton label.

When the collection came to light, some twenty five years ago, it had confidently been ascribed to WH Crome. This helps to illustrate the confusion over works of the school, making it all the more worthwhile to look at the six in some detail. As is so often the case with small paintings there are no signatures to see nor inscriptions to find. The paintings had been coupled together in pairs with matching frames a long time in the past.

The larger pair are comprised of the roadside cottage scene with a distant slender figure on horseback, and a painting of farm buildings. The road view has several JB Ladbrooke features, perhaps the chief one being the dark oak tree on the roadside with its clearly angled branches and its splayed tufts of finger-like foliage. This make-up contrasts with the fine falling fronds of the trees opposite, where highlights in the upper reaches are visible – a point of note. Did JB have lime trees in mind, with the sun shining on their winged summer fruits? The patch of grass, half in the shadows by the roadside, planted by partly crosshatching the blades, and the spiked twigs in the bush above, a maple maybe, are further signs of JB's hand. Confident of the authorship of this painting it is not difficult to spot the telltale characteristics in the other. First it will be seen that the background colouring of the central clump of trees and the foliage shaping, in particular in front of the building, are strikingly similar to that of the oak tree in the first picture. The oil paints must surely have come off the same palette. There are off-putting elements too, but JB did these from time to time. The stark tree trunk, with its few spots of pale foliage springing from it, may have been put in as a finishing touch, or even an afterthought. It helps to break the painting up and 'frame' the farm building with its pointed roof, which the tree spread above it also helps to do. Tucked away in the bottom corner by the rustic bridge, half hidden down a ditch, springs a cluster of leafy growth, detail he always liked to portray if he could. Sometimes this motif of his is almost like a signature – when it is more clearly visible!

The middle pair, with their fine frames, are of more interest because one holds a known Ladbrooke background and the other portrays, with its windmill, a less familiar heathland scene. In the Norwich Castle Museum there is an upright version of the cottage scene but without the horse and cart. That particular composition is varied a bit but otherwise contains the same basic elements. However this cart scene is a much more colourful and successful composition. There is fine subtle detail to be seen in the grasses on the bank beneath the silver birch tree. JB Ladbrooke, incidentally, often painted silver birches which must have been found widely in Norfolk. The thin and long leafy-green brush strokes of this tree, and the bush opposite, have been done with greater delicacy than was the fashion in his later and larger paintings where this foliage is quite frequently found. This little lane scene is carefully composed and balanced

Roadside Cottage. Oil on oak
panel. **JB Ladbrooke**
8 3/4 x 11 1/2 ins., 22.3 x 29.3 cms.

Farmstead. Oil on millboard.
JB Ladbrooke
9 1/8 x 12 ins., 23.2 x 30.5 cms.

Horse and Cart by a Cottage. Oil on oak panel.
JB Ladbrooke
6 ⁵⁄₈ x 9 ¹⁄₄ ins., 16.8 x 23.5 cms.

with its bank on one side and cottage on the other; the eye is attracted to the centre to rest on the cart where, comfortably, the figure sits on one side. This, the most absorbing painting of the set, shows JB at his best. It is interesting now to compare the immediate foreground of the lane scene with that of the heath scene for, although the subjects are different, the structure of this part is broadly similar both in colour and content. To see what is meant it is helpful to cover up both the paintings, except for the bottom inch on each, and then to compare what is left to view.

It is not generally realised that JB Ladbrooke painted many heath scenes, some of which show a rather darkly featured windmill such as this. Often the distant view in these shows a church on the horizon – in a dark colour, blue, where the horizon is bright. Some of the heath scenes, which tended to be among his earlier landscapes, show rocks, and in this little painting there is a small group placed so as to catch the low sunlight. In some of his early to mid period landscapes he used white paint, which he employed here, as if to show mist on distant meadowland. A glance at one or two others of this collection shows white on a roof top or tree trunk too. Many Norwich School paintings, such as this, pose a question or tell a tale. Is this the miller's wife out in the early morning, or could it be evening with her figure caught between long shadows making her way home? But, whatever the time of day, the clever use of light and dark gives depth and distinction to a flat landscape so typical of Norfolk – its customary church tower far away on the distant horizon.

Heathland with Windmill. Oil on millboard.
JB Ladbrooke
7 x 9 ins., 17.7 x 22.9 cms.

The final pair, though much smaller, merit fair comment as well. One is very different from the other. The wooded scene with tall trees is reminiscent of other small detailed landscapes, which in the past have gone unrecognised due to unfamiliarity with subject matter of this type and size; they have normally been attributed to SD Colkett, who was anyway a bit of a copyist. This painting has small fingers of cumulus cloud rising in the sky above another church. This feature of cloud 'fingers' is very much evident in JB's earlier works, though distant church towers go on appearing for many years. Perhaps he could not erase them from his memory after completing the task of recording the churches of Norfolk with his father! The other painting, of a cottage by a pond, is in some respects the most striking of the six for the manner in which the cottage stands out by reflecting brightness before a retreating storm. This is a sight with which we are all familiar when a passing rainfall has given way to summer sunshine glistening on freshly washed walls. The contrast lasts only so long as the storm beyond survives. JB Ladbrooke knew how to capture this moment. The actual subject, a cottage surrounded by trees and water, is typical of what he might have found on his travels through Norfolk with his father. Indeed the path he painted might have been the very one they trod together passing from parish to parish.

It may be noticed that all six views show a pathway of sorts. Perhaps this rare collection represents a glimpse into a picturesque diary of his much-travelled life through the Norfolk countryside.

Track to the Church. Oil on millboard. **JB Ladbrooke** 5 3/4 x 8 ins., 14.7 x 20.3 cms.

Cottage by a Pond. Oil on board. **JB Ladbrooke**
5 3/4 x 8 1/8 ins., 14.6 x 20.7 cms.

The Sluice Gate. Oil on canvas. **JB Ladbrooke**
17 x 23 ins., 43.2 x 58.4cms.
*This view was probably painted in the 1840s, after
seeing J Stark's 'Eel bucks on the Thames at Goring'.
WJ Muller painted the same view as Stark in 1843,
one artist probably inspiring the other, and then JBL
took his cue from them in his simplified versions –
two exist, the other without a figure. The trees show
dabs of deep blue in the high reaches, the same colour
as the distant horizon. A sienna bush, a field maple
perhaps, suggests the start of autumn – JB's favourite
time of year.*

Country Cottage. Watercolour. **R Dixon**
8 ¹/₄ x 11 ⁵/₈ ins., 20.9 x 29.6 cms.
*A typical Dixon domestic scene – he produced
many cottage views with figures of this kind,
rounding off his trees with foliage looking
something like little balls of wool painted in
watercolour.*

Ten
Ready reference

Fifty of the best known names associated
with the Norwich School
Book study • Bibliography

1 **Henry Bright (1810–1873)** Suffolk born, this painter of detail found marvellous mountain views at home and abroad. Specialised, too, in wide open sky-lit landscapes. Worked in oils, pastels, watercolours and pencil. Many pictures of boats, barns and other buildings. Numbers signed.

2 **James Bulwer (1794–1879)** Friend and pupil of JS Cotman. Topographical watercolourist and draughtsman. Pleasing views of Norfolk houses. Formed a collection of Norfolk church studies by Norwich artists.

3 **Joseph Clover (1779–1853)** Civic portrait painter, also produced landscapes in watercolour and oils in a fairly distinctive style. Landscape works quite rare, sometimes unrecognised.

4 **Samuel David Colkett (c1808–1863)** Notable pupil of James Stark, copied many of his works. Also influenced by G Vincent whose style he sometimes adopted. Prolific painter with many easy colourful landscapes to enjoy. Moved from Norwich to Yarmouth, then Cambridge. Often signed – pencil sketches, oils and watercolours.

5 **Edwin Cooper (1785–1833)** Painter of animals, horses and dogs, producing many drawings in eighteenth century style. Some horse and hound hunting scenes of high quality. Many works signed. Dog paintings lovely.

6 **John Sell Cotman (1782–1842)** Brilliant artist of international repute, ahead of his day with impressionist look. He generated the smaller stream of painters in the Norwich School, including his family, Thirtle and Priest, who took up some of his influence. Much already written about him over past one hundred years.

7 **Miles Edmund Cotman (1810–1858)** Like his father produced land and seascapes of fine quality, helped him to teach in Norwich and London. Early style is similar and sometimes confused with him. Occasionally signed.

8 **John Joseph Cotman (1814–1878)** Brother of ME Cotman. Fine draughtsman and watercolourist, excelled in the use of colour. Some very rich and romantic oil paintings, beautifully composed. Watercolours quite common, oils rare. Often signed.

9 **John Crome (1768–1821)** Father of the Norwich School, teacher of many. Drawing master at Norwich Grammar School. Influenced by Dutch Masters became an outstanding landscape painter making use of light with inspiring works. Usually unsigned. Several of his children painted, Frederick and Emily (ruined building in Castle Museum) are less known.

10 **John Berney Crome (1794–1842)** Referred to as 'Moonlight Crome'. Taught by his father, influenced by G Vincent, with whom he travelled. Many large landscapes, including night 'water' views, usually unsigned. Became bankrupt, moved from Norwich to Yarmouth.

11 **William Henry Crome (1806–1867)** Artist of moderate talent, lived and painted in many parts of British Isles. Green was his favourite colour, sometimes brightly used. Not as ambitious as his brother, cottages in landscapes best, mostly unsigned.

12 **Edward Thomas Daniell (1804–1842)** Landscape painter in watercolour and oils. Painted in Middle East. Produced quality etchings of scenes around Norwich.

13 **Robert Dixon (1780–1815)** Watercolour painter who enjoyed rendering roadside cottage scenes, some large ones of great merit, and beach scenes in somewhat primitive style. Etcher. Some works signed.

14 **William Freeman (1784–1877)** Like his father, Jeremiah (c1763–1823), exhibited landscapes and sea pieces with the Norwich Society, both were members, and framemakers besides.

St Benedict's Abbey. Oil on oak panel. **O Short**
4 5/8 x 8 1/2 ins., 11.7 x 21.6 cms.
The most painted ancient monument in Norfolk! A community lived on the island on the Broads for over 200 years before Canute in 1020 formed it into a mitred Benedictine abbey. Because of its situation it was known as St Benedict's de Hulmo (of the holm or island). Eventually the abbey enclosed an area of 30 acres. There was only one entrance, and all that remains, still to be seen, is the gate house which Obadiah Short and others painted.

Trowse Lane. Watercolour. **O Short**, inscribed with location
7 1/2 x 16 3/4 ins., 19 x 42.5 cms.
There is something of ME Cotman's influence here. The cows, slug-like, are recognisable as belonging to Obadiah, the squat cottages a further reminder. He exhibited few of his many paintings.

15 **William Philip Barnes Freeman (1813–1897)** Watercolour and oil painter picked out by easily recognisable spotty foliage in unexciting landscapes. Better with seascapes, some medium sized beautiful watercolours. Usually unsigned. Third generation of Freeman painting and frame making family.

16 **Joseph Geldhart (1808–1882)** Amateur artist who drew with a Cotman influence. Landscapes and portraits with effective use of chalk. One or two landscapes in oils. Sketched on the Continent.

17 **Charles Hodgson (1769–1856)** Oil and watercolour painter of landscape, and cathedral and church interiors. Architectural draughtsman. Interesting painter who influenced his son David. Few works to study.

18 **David Hodgson (1798–1864)** Most distinctive style and use of colour in his town views of Norwich, Chester and elsewhere. Painter of landscapes, churches and cathedrals – inside and outside. Best at timber framed buildings with overhanging gables. Some works signed.

19 **William Joy (1803–1867)** and

20 **John Cantiloe Joy (c1806–c1866)** Both born in Yarmouth. William seems to have been the busier artist with fine watercolours and oils. Specialised in seascapes, William produced a few fine landscapes. Storm scenes at sea, or rescues, particularly impressive. Some good sized works often unsigned. Moved away to Portsmouth and new shipping scenes with men-of-war.

21 **Henry Jutsum (1816–1869)** On the fringe, but heavily influenced by H Bright and a pupil of J Stark. Oils and watercolours have some flavour of the Norwich School. A pleasing artist, many works signed.

22 **Robert Ladbrooke (1769–1842)** Friend of John Crome. Painted many landscapes, early ones in dark tones. Detailed panoramic views of Norwich in particular. Later works much brighter (possibly son Robert's work or even grandson's). Made complete record, with JBL, of all Norfolk's churches. Eldest son, Robert, became a framer, the rest artists.

23 **Henry Ladbrooke (1800–1869)** Detailed landscape painter, trees his favourite subject, a pupil of Crome. Taught in many Norfolk towns. Colourful artist who completed some large canvases. Works often unsigned. Views later in life around hometown Kings Lynn.

24 **John Berney Ladbrooke (1803–1879)** Prolific and gifted painter mainly in oils, some watercolours, many pencil drawings. Studied under Crome, visited different parts of Britain. Extensive use of colour, many works unsigned, some a fair size.

25 **Frederick Ladbrooke (1810–1865)** Half-brother to other Ladbrookes, moved to Bury St Edmunds. Friend and colleague of ER Smythe. Painted landscapes and portraits. Little available for study, mostly unsigned.

26 **Robert Leman (1799–1863)** Competent watercolourist with small and large views. Liked to study trees; his buildings were richly coloured with red-brown brickwork.

27 **Edward Littlewood (fl.1863–1896)** Produced many oils with style and colouring of JB Ladbrooke who probably taught him. Some completely mimic JB. A minor watercolourist. Works common, many signed. A school follower.

28 **Thomas Lound (1802–1861)** Said to be an amateur, but very good and interesting. Fine watercolours of Broads and Fens. Oils can be beautifully atmospheric. Influenced by David Cox. Usually unsigned. Etcher.

29 **Horace Beevor Love (1800–1838)** Top quality watercolour portraits, often in semi-miniature, with deft touches. Painted a number of small landscapes. Rarely seen. Some works signed. Born in Norwich, painted members of the School.

Sheep in a Lane. Oil on canvas. **O Short**, signed
and dated 1876
9 1/2 x 13 3/8 ins., 24 x 34 cms.
*Obadiah painted many pictures in later life,
often with a busy flock of sheep on the move.
He was an amateur artist who once looked to
JB Ladbrooke for instruction; his influence
shows in early paintings, but not so much in
later ones.*

Postwick Grove. Oil on millboard. **O Short**
9 7/8 x 14 1/8 ins., 25.1 x 35.9 cms.
*Inspired by Stark's version of one of the most
popular locations Obadiah produced this one
with heifers testing the water! One looks
rather unhappy.*

117

30 **Maria Margitson (1832–1896)** Niece of JB Ladbrooke, specialised in still life. Subject matter similar to EH Stannard, not of same quality. Works not uncommon.

31 **John Middleton (1827–1856)** Artist of great merit who excelled in wooded landscapes in oil and watercolour, influenced by H Bright his teacher. Fine views of streams and lanes, some a good size and some signed. Died young.

32 **John Ninham (1754–1817)** Little known artist, specialised in trade painting, never became member of Norwich Society. Characteristically an eighteenth century painter who made several views of Norwich.

33 **Henry Ninham (1796–1874)** Son of John Ninham. Long lived recorder of many town and river views in Norwich. Distinctive style. Printer and etcher. Street life views particularly interesting. Usually unsigned.

34 **Joseph Paul (1804–1887)** Rather unpleasing heavy style of landscape painting at times. Copied J Crome's work. Some small moonlights and landscapes quite attractive. Works common but rarely, if ever, signed. Moved to London.

35 **John Paul (1847–1900)** Son of Joseph. Began painting horses in landscapes. Principally known for his later London views and therefore not confused with his father. The latter are seen quite commonly, but the horses are rare.

36 **Alfred Priest (1810–1850)** Oil and watercolour painter of landscapes and marines, some with Cotman influence. Also produced a number of charming small landscapes, some tiny. Pupil of J Stark when living in London. Etcher. Some works signed.

37 **Anthony Sandys (1806–1883)** A portrait painter, then a landscape one. Many brightly lit views in the Crome idiom around Norfolk, often with wherries and windmills. Some paintings initialled or monogrammed.

38 **Obadiah Short (1803–1886)** Landscape painter, oils influenced by JB Ladbrooke, early paintings in his style. More loosely painted scenes later, often of lanes. Minor artist who sometimes signed.

39 **James Sillett (1764–1840)** Competent painter of town views, landscapes, still life and miniature portraits. Probably studied Dutch flower pieces to produce his own examples. Oils and watercolours, sometimes signed.

40 **Joseph Stannard (1797–1830)** Fine artist who produced beautiful river and shore scenes and seascapes. Visited Holland. Superb draughtsman and etcher. Brother Alfred's best shipping scenes sometimes confused with his. Master of the School.

41 **Alfred Stannard (1806–1889)** Oil painter of great quality in mid-period, large detailed landscapes and river scenes in particular. Used lovely colours. Like his brother, Joseph, painted shore scenes and seascapes. Often unsigned, especially small ones.

42 **Emily Stannard (1803–1885)** Wife of Joseph, née Coppin. Detailed flower pieces with beautiful colours and a Dutch influence reveal her best potential. Dead game and fish are less attractive but characteristically superb. Works not uncommon, a number signed.

43 **Eloise Harriet Stannard (1829–1915)** Daughter of Alfred. Long lived prolific painter of still life for which she is well known. Elaborate colourful compositions of fruit, flowers and insects. Large output, often signed and dated.

44 **Alfred George Stannard (1828–1885)** Son of Alfred. Landscape painter with numbers of sea pieces. Trees show a late Norwich style blending into a Victorian one. Some very attractive and competent small views. Sometimes signed.

45 **Anna Maria Stannard (1828–post 1885)** Wife of Alfred George and daughter of D Hodgson. Accomplished painter of still life who used Emily Stannard as her model.

Sunken Lane. Oil on mahogany panel. **O Short**
5 7/8 x 4 5/8 ins., 14.9 x 11.7 cms.
Wayside bushy trees in a scene not unlike Priest's small glade painting. This is one of a collection of half a dozen Shorts recently discovered – 'St Benet's' and a 'Wooded Lane' being the other two illustrated. It is exactly as found, discoloured by ageing varnish.

Wooded Lane. Oil on oak panel. **O Short**, signed
7 1/4 x 10 5/8 ins., 18.4 x 27 cms.
Touches of grey paint sometimes mark Obadiah's trees. A gnarled oak is a reminder of JB Ladbrooke's influence. He signed more of his later works than early ones, but even then not very often.

46 James Stark (1794–1859) Fine artist, prolific pupil of Crome and the RA. Early wooded landscapes belong to his Norwich period, later ones to the Windsor era style. All sizes, usually unsigned, a collection of which were engraved for 'Scenery of the Rivers of Norfolk'.

47 Arthur James Stark (1831–1902) On the fringe, a landscape painter influenced by his father. Norfolk subjects in oils and watercolour, later paintings in many parts of England. Specialised in animals, enjoyed farm scenes. A number signed.

48 John Thirtle (1777–1839) Very fine watercolourist, delighted in town and river scenes around Norwich. Animated painter who produced quality work, early on reminiscent of Girtin. Wrote a treatise on watercolour, ran a framing business. Works rare, usually unsigned.

49 George Vincent (1796–1832) Brilliant oil painter, pupil of Crome. Produced small and very large paintings, and a few superb etchings. Fine use of colour, arguably Crome's finest pupil. Some works signed with initials or name. Debts sent him to the Fleet Prison in London.

50 Cornelius Jansen Walter Winter (1817–1891) Painter of horses, farm scenes and landscapes, some in Bungay area. Miniaturist. Father of Rowland (Holmes) Winter. The few works seen outside the museum are signed. Completed hundreds of watercolours of church art for Bulwer.

Book study

The Norwich School of Painting *WF Dickes*

This book must be described as the 'Bible' of the Norwich School. In his introduction Dickes writes of the painters and paintings:

> *Uninfluenced by prescription or tradition, but surrounded by scenes of a special sort, with the delightful features they could not help being in love, they boldly declared NATURE THEIR ONLY GUIDE. And, when they founded their Society and held exhibitions of their works, it soon became evident to the world that their Art was distinguished by a speciality. Love of their native heathland, rivers, mills, and woods had kept them so continually repeating the same views under every change of sunshine and shadow – their palettes were so constantly set with the same rich and mellow colours – that even when they went to other scenes their colouring and touch declared them still 'of Norwich'.*

The six hundred pages of the masterpiece are well illustrated with 170 pictures. The comprehensive text is crammed with detail, but half the book is devoted to John Crome and John Sell Cotman, leaving the other half to cover many artists. It is a most useful reference book.

Dickes ends: 'If the Norwich School be now a memory of the past, its teaching has become the inheritance, and a distinguishing feature, of all British Art.'

Only 500 were printed of which 100 were a special edition. The ordinary one once sold for two guineas. Today it sells for what would be 300 guineas, or more.

Northrepps Road, Cromer. Oil on panel. **O Short**
10 $^1/_2$ x 13 ins., 26.7 x 33 cms.
The likely location of this painting came to light with the discovery of a pencil drawing depicting the same scene, an inscription on its mount. The oil painting was attributed to O Short by the late Alec Cotman of the Castle Museum. H Ladbrooke also painted this subject; he may have inspired Short to follow him as the cloud formation is one of HL's early types. The Cromer painting, by its quaintness, looks early too.

ENGLISH SCHOOL
Northrepps Road, Cromer. Pencil drawing.
Early 19th century, inscription on mount, artist unknown.
3 $^5/_8$ x 4 $^3/_8$ ins., 9.1 x 11.3 cms.
This drawing of Cromer is included for the reason that it gives the location of one of O Short's paintings. Many Norwich School paintings are 'identified' by reference to another picture – in or out of the school.

121

The Norwich School of Painters *Miklos Rajnai*

For a quick ready reference to the Norwich School this 32 page 'soft back' beats every-thing else. It is packed with detail and many well chosen paintings. It is an easy book to use and, following an introduction, runs briefly through 32 artists – all illustrated bar one. This is done roughly in order of birth, which gives the advantage that by flipping through the pages the reader can observe how the painting styles varied over the seven decades of the School's life.

Watercolours of the Norwich School *Derek Clifford*

A worthy and most erudite text which goes into a lot of detail about the artists. Over 150 black and white quality photographs and eight colour plates. These cover 50 artists of which about 30 are well remembered Norwich School names. A quarter of the plates cover John Crome and John Sell Cotman. The greater number of illustrations had not been published before 1965. About 100 of them are taken from museums or public buildings.

East Anglian Painters Vol II and III *Harold Day*

These two volumes, par excellence, can be considered to have promoted the Norwich School more than any other written work since the publication of Dickes' book in 1905. They revealed on their publication a wealth of previously unseen material spanning all the well known members of the School. No other publication, before or since, has achieved such a feat. Though time has taken its toll, by there being better reproduction facilities thirty years on, the black and white illustrations, many of full page size, show excellent detail. The choice of illustrations has meant that minor but delightful artists were included for the first time. The text on artists is seriously concise and covers all the salient points ending with a description of the artist's works. Lists of the artist's exhibits follow with dates, and sometimes, with the death of an artist, there is even a list of effects in relation to the contents of his private picture collection, as put up for sale or whatever.

The books were published at a time when many Norwich School paintings began tumbling on to the market. Armed with these books a collector at last had a chance to gain an armchair knowledge when sallying forth. Today they still provide for the need they set out to fulfil and the original volumes represent a first choice for any collector. If the portraits of each artist, which precede each chapter are excluded, the two volumes then contain just over 200 illustrations with a small handful in colour. Eighty of these come from public collections, mostly the Norwich Castle Museum. The plates in the original volumes are slightly better than in the reprints. These first volumes were limited to 1,000 copies and are not uncommonly found in secondhand book shops, especially in East Anglia.

The Norwich School, Crome, Cotman and their followers *Huon Mallalieu*

This eighty page book contains a fair number of Castle Museum pictures amongst its almost 80 illustrations. It is a useful handbook, considering Norwich artists individually and by families – there are brief notes devoted to the Cotmans (though John Sell has an illustrated chapter to himself), the Hodgsons, Ladbrookes, Starks, and the Stannards. By modern standards the quality of the black and white illustrations leaves a little to be desired, besides which many of the paintings appear in other books.

The Norwich School of Painters 1803–1833 *Andrew Hemingway*

This book will be known for its fine colour reproduction of some important Norwich School paintings. The 80 pages contain nearly 70 plates carefully spread amongst the text which concentrates on the artists' styles together with ample history of the members of the school. Some of the colour pictures stand out – in particular two early pictures by James Stark ('Penning the Flock' and 'A Wooded Landscape') which are placed alongside useful detail in the text of the artist's style in his formative years. The last two book illustrations, a panoramic view of Cromer by Thirtle and a barn interior by ME Cotman, make a fine ending.

The Norwich School of Artists *A Moore*

This is a modern day textbook on the Norwich School, usefully dividing the school up into different classes. There is a three part section on Crome, Crome's pupils and Crome's contemporaries. There are two chapters on Cotman and his pupils and his friends. This is followed by the Stannard family and the Joy brothers. The concluding chapters are on second generation and younger artists. These divisions greatly simplify the study of the school and make it easier to absorb the excellent detail provided. Most of the illustrations are gleaned from the Castle collection and number 167, of which three dozen are portraits, many of these being small margin inserts of the artists themselves. Thirty two illustrations are in colour, with some of these paintings permanently on view in the Castle galleries.

A Country Parson *from James Woodforde's diary*

This book uses the Norwich School as a source of illustration. For this purpose alone the cross section of the School given by 40 colour pictures is admirable.

The Williams Family of Painters *Jan Reynolds*

An immensely valuable book to have standing alongside any Norwich School book collection with 170 black and white illustrations and a handful of colour ones. Many of these portray fine woodland landscapes and river scenes. The generous size of plates allows for easy comparisons between the Williams' styles of painting and those of the Norwich School.

Dutch Painters of the Nineteenth Century (Marius)
edited by Geraldine Norman

This book was first published in Dutch in 1903, and therefore about the same time as Dickes' book, and later in English in 1908. With the more recent addition of a large number of extra illustrations in an addendum, it makes for a first class introduction to Dutch painting of that era. Much is written about the Hague School. From 275 illustrations an appreciation of nineteenth century painting can be gathered on a grand scale. This basic work of references by GH Marius (with additions), like Dickes' book of its time, is a most enjoyable book to handle. Copies appear from time to time in secondhand book shops.